Fisher Press

PEARL OF GREAT PRICE

Antony Matthew was born in London in 1936. As a child he went with his family to Sarawak during the Second World War. When the Japanese invaded Borneo, the family settled in Perth, Western Australia, while his father served in the Australian army. After the War he went to Geelong Grammar School during the Headmastership of Sir James Darling. He read Classics at Melbourne University, then Social Anthropology at Cambridge where Sir Edmund Leach was his supervisor. He joined the Foreign Office in 1962. He had two tours in London and one at the British Embassy in Senegal, where he acted briefly as Chargé d'Affaires. He was posted as Head of Chancery to the British Embassy in Belgrade in 1972, but resigned to broaden his experience in merchant banking. After training with Lazards his career in finance took him to New York and Melbourne. He rejoined the British Civil Service in 1976. He was received as a Catholic in Brixton on the Feast of the Visitation in 1985. He is married with a daughter and a son.

To Mary

ANTONY MATTHEW

PEARL OF GREAT PRICE

Becoming a Catholic - A practical guide

Illustrated by Mary Tyler

...Again the Kingdom of Heaven is like unto a merchant man, seeking goodly pearls: Who when he had found one pearl of great price, went and sold all that he had and bought it.

St Matthew, Chapter 13, verses 45-46
in *The Authorised Version of the Bible*

Fisher Press

Published by Fisher Press, Post Office Box 41,
Sevenoaks, Kent TN15 6YN, England

Pearl of Great Price first published 1991
First issued as a Fisher paperback 1991

British Library Cataloguing in Publication Data
A catalogue record for this book is available from
The British Library.

ISBN 1 874037 01 9

Typeset by Computer Techniques, Kemsing, Kent
Printed by Antony Rowe Ltd. Chippenham, Wiltshire
Cover: Brown Knight & Truscott Ltd, Tunbridge Wells, Kent

CONTENTS

ACKNOWLEDGEMENTS

My thanks are due to the Catholic Truth Society for permission to quote from *A Catechism of Christian Doctrine*, which is approved by the Archbishops and Bishops of England and Wales; and to make reference to other publications of theirs including *A Simple Prayer Book*, and *Order of the Mass in Latin and English*. I am also grateful to Monsignor Gilbey and to Mrs Cecilia Bevan for their permission to refer to *We Believe* and *A Book of Catholic Prayers* respectively. I owe a special debt of gratitude to the Rev Hugh Thwaites SJ. His six audio-cassette recordings, in which he comments on *A Catechism of Christian Doctrine*, have been invaluable; in so many ways he was a special channel for God's grace for me. The opening quotation from the *Authorised Version of the Bible*, the rights in which are vested in the Crown, is reproduced by kind permission of the Crown's patentees, Cambridge University Press. I am also very grateful to a number of priests and others who have read and commented on parts or all of the typescript from their different perspectives. Its remaining sins of commission and omission are all mine. Special thanks are also due to the owner of E J Lambert's watercolour of the interior of the Brompton Oratory for permission to use it for the design of the cover of this book.

PREFACE

MUCH of my life has been spent travelling in one way or another. I was born in London, but before I was four years old, I went with my mother and brother to join my father in Sarawak. He had gone out to this part of Borneo before the Second World War to work as a geologist. He thought we would be safer there than amid the bombs on London. We went by sea. Our ship became separated from its protective convoy of warships, and we had some narrow escapes from German submarines. After a voyage of many weeks we managed to meet my father safely in Sarawak's little capital, Kuching.

My father was always a traveller. He was abroad when both my brother and I were born. I suspect that he took up geology because it gave him scope for an adventurous life. He made expeditions over much of East Africa, established a mine among the wild Karens of Northern Burma, and prospected for minerals in other parts of South-East Asia as well as Borneo. He had been an officer in the British Royal Flying Corps in the 1914-18 War. But it was characteristic of him to volunteer as a private in the Australian army when Japan entered the Second World War. Since he was to be based in Australia, the family were sent on to

Western Australia when Borneo was invaded by the Japanese.

While my father was away at the War, I was sent to a local State primary school near Perth. I believe he did this out of principle; its rather rough style would help me adapt more quickly to Australian ways than a school where parents paid fees for refinement in their children. But I imagine that at that time his private's pay meant he couldn't really have afforded to do otherwise. I walked the mile or so to school. The girls wore shoes, but it was not the custom for the boys, so I learned to go without them.

After the war we went to live thirty-five miles outside Canberra, where my father managed a mine. The mining settlement was remote from local secondary schools, and, as I was now eleven and our fortunes had improved, it was decided I should go away to boarding school in Victoria. There I was given elocution lessons to modify the strong Western Australian accent I had by now developed.

At the end of each term it took me almost a whole day to make the journey home. I had to travel by bus, train, an old-fashioned Melbourne tram, an airline coach, a DC3 æroplane, then by car along the dusty gravel road to the mine. I was always terrified of losing one of the many tickets I needed. Later, as a young man, I made the long sea voyage back again to Britain to attend university.

A career in the British Foreign Service meant further travel. My wife and I were posted to West Africa. Later I worked briefly on Wall Street in New York as a banker. Back in Australia, banking was still my line in Melbourne. But my wife and I spent a lot of time running a small holding in the country. In recent years I have had a job in the British Civil Service. This has involved more travel: in Britain and Europe.

Looking back on all this to-ing and fro-ing, I now

see that there was one recurring theme which was significant for my spiritual journey: wherever I travelled, I visited churches, private chapels, cathedrals and monasteries. As it happened, most of these belonged to the great Catholic tradition of Christendom. For many years I was just a tourist, looking at what was beautiful to my eye, or of historical interest. Somehow I did not associate what I saw with religion at all. Nor did I reflect on the underlying motives of the architects, artists and patrons who had built or embellished the buildings.

Nor, during all these visits, do I consciously remember noticing my fellow human beings, or reflecting on the reasons why they might also be there. It was a long time before this strange mist before my eyes cleared. Then, gradually, I began to notice them too. And there they were, as they always had been: kneeling on the imported Italian marble pavement of an Australian cathedral in an old gold mining town, or on rush matting in a wooden church in the Casamance in Senegal, or before the tabernacle in the ambulatory chapel of some baroque monastic church: praying quietly, or lighting candles, saying their rosary, or making the Stations of the Cross. Some were sitting patiently on benches waiting their turn to enter the confessional box.

I began to be aware of something mysterious, yet powerfully attractive; and then to envy this strong assurance of Faith. For unlike me, these worshippers were in harmony with the purpose for which the buildings, and all that was in them, had been made. I have long suspected that others may, on occasion, have felt the same. But the moment for them often passes, without any decision to take the matter further. In this book I shall tell you what you might do to become a part of that great Catholic tradition of Christendom.

I am writing from my own experience as an Anglican

who became a Catholic. I hope that what I say will be of value to those who are already Christians, those of other religions, and those of no religious beliefs at all.

It is not my purpose to try to convince you of the truths of the Catholic Faith. I am not a theologian. There are plenty of wonderful books to help with this. They show how the Faith, which so many clever men and women throughout the ages have come to accept as true, is marvellously consistent with human reason. Yet because we are given free-will by God, the Faith cannot be proved by knock-down argument. When He created us, God did not want human beings to be like computers, each simply playing back a programme which He had devised for us. So He gave us the wonderful gift of free-will. But this means we have the awesome responsibility of making our own choices.

As I have learned, a person can only really be attracted towards the Faith, not compelled to accept it. The possibilities for Faith are all around us, in the grace which God is constantly pouring out on us all. My purpose in writing is to help you become aware of this grace, and to breathe deeply of it; and then to help you respond in a practical way, if you are drawn to it, and to tell how you might live an ordinary life as a Catholic, if you became one.

But remember, if you *do* become a Catholic, you will no longer be living an ordinary life. For you will have thrown open a window through which you will see a glimpse of heaven.

ANTONY MATTHEW
Strathglass, Inverness-shire, 1990.

Mapledurham House

CHAPTER ONE

ON THE THRESHOLD

IN the name of the Father, and of the Son, and of the Holy Spirit. I begin in this time-honoured way in the hope that I will be given the grace to bring to you what will be most helpful for your particular journey. As I need God's grace to assist me in writing this book, so you will need His grace if you are to become a Catholic. In the end all I can do is to encourage you to respond to the grace which God has been offering you ever since you were born.

You have decided to read this book. You are therefore already an enquirer into the Church. You may not yet know this but you are embarking on a marvellous adventure. This is only a tiny first step, but it can be a vital one. The destination of your journey is not certain. Only God, who is outside time, knows if you will become a Catholic here on earth. But what is sure is that when Our Lord Jesus Christ, God Himself, became a human being like us, He urged His disciples to go out into all the world and preach the Gospel to every nation. So anyone who is trying to encourage you to respond seriously to His grace, is simply following

His commands. This is both an exciting and humbling thought.

But why in these days of Christian ecumenism and of most welcome better understanding between Christians, and between those of other religious beliefs and Christians, should you become a Catholic? In the end there is only one reason: because it will be of great benefit for your soul. In the case of some converts, the soul, or inner being as some call this, appears to recognise this very quickly. But for others, their conversion was more like being tugged along, for what seemed like ages, by a very long fishing line. They themselves seemed to have very little ultimate control, except perhaps to vary the pace at which they were being pulled ashore. Whether or not you are conscious of what will be good for your soul, or you seem simply to be caught up in the powerful action of grace, it might be helpful to you if I tried to identify some of the symptoms.

If you are already a member of a Christian church you may have begun to find less joy in its church services and teachings. You are restless spiritually. Some days you feel elated, other days tremendously down. What seems to be being offered by your church seems an inadequate response to the extraordinary idea that God had actually become a human being in the person of Our Lord Jesus Christ.

Perhaps, on the other hand, you are a "born again" Christian. But you are beginning to question your Christian group's lack of authority for its interpretation of Sacred Scripture. When several good Christians disagree about what some passage in the Bible means, who is right? You may be concerned about what seems to you an over-emphasis on emotional experience, or perhaps over-reliance on a particularly powerful individual. Is this enough to sustain all the different types of ordinary human beings in good times and bad?

You may be troubled when a "born again" Christian seems to go off the rails. How can this be when he or she has been "saved", and what should be done to bring him or her back to a right relationship with God?

You may yourself begin to feel enormous guilt. For your minister, or the person responsible for you spiritually, may be a particularly good person, even a close personal friend. You may have started to feel that your Christian denomination is beginning to deviate from its true path, and that no one seems to be able to stop this happening. You may even sense that the original reasons why some of the Protestant churches separated from the Catholic Church many centuries ago, however justified they may have seemed at the time, were, in some fundamental way, flawed.

If you have never been a Christian at all you may be starting to feel, for no clearly obvious reason, that life seems more dull and unprofitable than usual. Before, you were reasonably well-satisfied with the sensual pleasures of life: eating and drinking, making love, bodily exercise, the simple joys of being with family and friends. You were previously getting enough out of your life from the development of your private interests or hobbies, from your job or profession; or from watching television, going to the cinema, the theatre or concerts; or from keeping up with international or local news, or sporting events. Now, none of this really satisfies. Even holidays seem to be no lasting cure.

If you pride yourself on being a determined non-believer, you may even be finding a loss of satisfaction in the uncompromising rigour of your agnosticism or atheism. Although you may have no concept of soul, and may deny even the possibility of the existence of anything non-material, yet you recognise that there is some kind of malaise in your innermost spirits.

Some of those in this condition will simply go to their doctor, and describe their condition in physical terms. Some doctors will offer you a palliative, or suggest counselling. I often wonder if some of those suffering from conditions caused by unknown viruses, may not in reality be in this situation. If you are very lucky, a doctor may perceive this as spiritual hunger. If nothing effective is done I have no doubt that some will actually develop physical symptoms. Sometimes these will even turn into illness. The New Testament shows the close links that can exist between physical illness and a person's spiritual condition.

Many of those who do successfully recognise that they have developed a spiritual sickness simply turn to whatever source of support there is to hand. The huge growth of interest in all forms of religion is evidence of this yearning. So is the response of publishing firms, which have issued so many books of different kinds to cater for it. But unless a person receives proper guidance at this stage he or she can easily fall a prey to whatever fashionable wind of doctrine or belief is currently blowing about strongly. As G K Chesterton has remarked, once people no longer believe in God, they do not believe in nothing, they believe in anything.

A word of counsel. The Catholic Church has existed since it was founded by Our Lord Jesus Christ almost two thousand years ago. Experience has shown that many of the possibilities on offer from churches or sects which have separated from loyalty to the successors of St Peter have simply got some perfectly good Christian principle or point of doctrine out of balance. Ronald Knox, in his book, *Enthusiasm*, provides a detailed account of the problems and disasters which can occur when particular aspects of Christian teaching are exaggerated.

Knox's book is full of Christian charity towards those caught up in these exaggerations. Their intentions were often so well-meaning. They were trying to correct what they saw as an abuse in the Church. But so often the new solution they introduced led to an even worse difficulty, although this may not have become apparent immediately. Knox shows, in great detail, what can actually happen when Christian groupings or sects separate themselves from the wisdom and experience which the Church has built up over the centuries, under the guidance of the Holy Spirit. For the Catholic Church's orthodoxy, and its balance, are guaranteed by Our Lord's commission to St Peter and his successors.

Of course St Peter's boat, as the Church is sometimes called, can sometimes be tossed about. Many of those in it are all too human, and this can include some of those who are steering its course. But the ultimate goal of the Church is assured. Our Lord made this clear, as the New Testament, which is God's inspired word, records.

In a situation of restlessness and confusion it is important to recognise that these symptoms are a sign of grace, a precious opportunity being offered us by God. Some agnostics may even find themselves wishing they could believe in Christianity. In these circumstances it is important to begin to resist the promptings of the enemy, who will try to encourage a person to treat this as an attack of feeble-mindedness.

In my own case, as a practising Anglican, this lethargy for all things connected with my church at the time, and for all the other aspects of my life which had previously absorbed me, was offset by the beginning of feverish activity. This took the form of seeking out and devouring everything relating directly or indirectly to the Catholic Faith.

For me, books by famous converts seemed particularly fascinating. Because of the historical Anglican prejudices against Catholics, I sometimes found myself taking a lot of trouble to conceal my passionate interest from friends and relations. Such writings had an almost illicit attraction. Anyone who has tried to discuss religion, particularly Catholicism, seriously with friends, without adequate preparation, and without the special grace provided by God for this, will usually learn that the anti-Catholic prejudices of the ordinary Briton are by no means dead. So when I began to acquire my passionate interest in Catholic writings, I had just a tiny glimpse of what it must have been like to read banned Christian writings in Rome at the time of the early Christian martyrs, or in Eastern Europe during the persecution of Christianity under Communism.

Inevitably I was drawn to the well-known conversion stories first. Cardinal Newman's *Apologia Pro Vita Sua* tells the story of his attempts to revitalise the Anglican church through the Oxford movement. He recounts how he gradually realised that the Catholic Church, despite all the changes which seemed to have occurred since the time of the apostles, was still the true Church Our Lord had founded, and which St Peter and his successors had kept on course. It is a captivating story. As a bonus it is told in Newman's magical prose. Newman had earlier simplified the story and presented it in a piece of imaginative literature. His novel, *Loss and Gain*, offers a compelling picture of an individual being captured by grace.

My quest went on. Shane Leslie's biography of Cardinal Manning tells how another brilliant young Anglican, already an archdeacon and mounting the Church of England's ecclesiastical ladder, became a Catholic; then, after many changes of fortune, an Archbishop and Cardinal. One book led me on to another. R H Benson's *Confessions of a Convert* tells of his spiritual journey from his childhood as the son of an Anglican Archbishop of Canterbury, through his ordination as an Anglican clergyman; and so to his conversion to Catholicism, and to his life as a Catholic priest. Benson spent his short life pouring out novels on Catholic themes, and devotional works, so as to bring his new found faith to others. The proceeds of his short, but enormously successful literary career, were used to buy a lovely country house, which he left in his will to the then Catholic Archbishop of Westminster. It is still used as a country retreat by the Archbishop's successor today.

There is almost a genre of autobiographical writing about conversion to the Catholic Faith: G K Chesterton's *Autobiography*, Ronald Knox's *Spiritual Æneid*, Vernon Johnson's *One Lord, One Faith*, Evelyn Waugh's *A Little Learning*, Malcolm Muggeridge's *Conversion- A Spiritual Journey*. A particularly touching recent example is Alec Guiness' autobiography, *Blessings in Disguise*. Indeed, when John Mortimer noted that so many good modern writers were Catholics, Muriel Spark, another Catholic convert, felt it necessary to warn writers against becoming a Catholic merely to improve their prose style!

But I felt that my hunger was not completely satisfied with reading these classic autobiographical accounts of literary figures. I began to take an interest in the religious beliefs and achievements of others I admired, who I now discovered had been Catholics. This began to give me what I saw as new insight into what they were trying to achieve. Obviously most mediæval and renaissance art, writing and music, now began to be seen from a new angle. But I even began to read poets like Dryden and Pope with what seemed to be new understanding. Previously they had seemed indistinguishable from their seventeenth and eighteenth century contemporaries. Now I saw something which linked them together and set them apart.

I even began to devour the poems of that mystic vagrant Francis Thompson. Previously his book of collected verse had been all but abandoned on the bookshelf, since I had received a finely bound edition as a school prize. Before it had seemed too strange, even mawkish. Now it all seemed so different:

> The angels keep their ancient places;—
> Turn but a stone, and start a wing!
> 'Tis ye, 'tis your estrangèd faces,
> That miss the many-splendoured thing.
>
> But (when so sad thou canst not sadder)
> Cry; — and upon thy so sore loss
> Shall shine the traffic of Jacob's ladder
> Pitched between Heaven and Charing Cross.

I had always been thrilled by the passion and grandeur of Bruckner's symphonies. Once I had myself become closer to an understanding of his Catholic Faith, his musical ideas seemed even more compelling, and the links between his sacred and symphonic music more intelligible. I vowed a pilgrimage to the Augustinian abbey of St Florian in Upper Austria where he had been a devoted organist—a vow I have only recently fulfilled on the Feast of the Ascension. The reasons for the mystical yearning in the music of César Franck seemed more apparent. Even the music of Lizst, for which I had no instinctive attraction, now came to have new meaning, especially his church music, and the music he wrote in Rome, or at the Villa d'Este.

Among the musicians of this century I discovered Poulenc. At a time when I had almost lost my ability to concentrate on opera, a former love, and one which had become almost a substitute for religion for many of my contemporaries, I was enthralled by his opera, *The Dialogue of the Carmelites*. This tells of the martyrdom of a convent of nuns during the French Revolution.

It was not only in music that I extended my pursuit

of Catholic tradition across the Channel. I sought out the work of that great passionate band of modern French Catholics: Paul Claudel, George Bernanos and the film director, Robert Bresson. I soon discovered that I had a companion in this pursuit. He was as fascinated as I was by them: the English actor, Robert Speaight. He had developed a parallel career to his acting, by writing biographies of French Catholic writers and thinkers in English; so drawing their life and work to the attention of English speakers. Another convert to the Catholic Faith, Speaight has set out the story of his own journey in his autobiography, *The Property Basket.*

As was perhaps inevitable, I began to listen to the music of Edward Elgar in a different way. *The Dream of Gerontius* seemed even more awesome now that I was beginning to understand the Faith in which it was written. When the work was first taken to Moscow in the 1980s, before perestroika, the Soviet Ministry of Culture would not allow Cardinal Newman's text of the sacred drama to be printed in the programme, or for there to be any explanation of what the work was about. I could now understand their thinking: æsthetic pleasure was permissible, but no risk was to be taken at the time that ordinary Russians should be consciously contaminated with the Christian Faith which the work so poignantly expresses!

In architecture, I began to look more closely not only at the great mediæval cathedrals, abbeys and churches, which I had previously admired as a tourist. But I sought out those designed by the two Pugins, by J F Bentley, who designed Westminster Cathedral, and the buildings, especially the churches, of Harcourt Rendell.

As a keen gardener I remember the extraordinary excitement I felt when I discovered that Major Lawrence Johnston, the creator of Hidcote Manor, the great Cotswold garden, which had such a profound influence on Vita Sackville-West's and Harold Nicholson's garden at Sissinghurst, was a Catholic.

I have no doubt that if others had been aware of this feverish collecting of Catholics with some worldly reputation, they would have pronounced me obsessed. But my quest and passion were private. At last I had begun to discover some secret power behind a creativity I had previously admired, but only half understood. Now I knew what this vital element was.

I often felt obliged to conceal the special excitement I felt when visiting the great houses of those families which had remained loyal to the Old Faith: Oxburgh, Stonor, Mapledurham, Sawston Hall; Baddesley Clinton, Coughton Court, Traquair in Scotland, Arundel Castle. Their names still ring in my ears like a great litany.

I found the lonely ruin of Lyveden New Bield in Northamptonshire particularly moving. Sir Thomas Tresham had built this small country house in the late sixteenth century to honour Our Lord and His Blessed Mother. Around the outside walls he had had a frieze placed depicting the symbols of Our Lord's passion. There were also texts from Sacred Scripture and the Holy Mass in Latin. Despite its situation in a remote part of the county, it was an extraordinarily brave thing to do at a time when the Catholic Faith was being severely persecuted in the last years of Queen Elizabeth's reign.

Disaster struck the family before the building was completed. Sir Thomas' son, Francis, was held to be implicated in the Gunpowder Plot. He was brought to trial with the others, convicted, then hanged, drawn and quartered. The house was probably never completed. It stands as a beautiful ruin, a memorial to one man's loyalty to Our Lord and His Church in a time of persecution.

Another feature of my symptoms was an awareness of a pattern of seemingly odd but meaningful coincidences: unexpected meetings with people, tiny items in the newspaper, a few words on the radio or television: all of them seemed to link together, and draw attention to the Catholic Faith.

If you experience this condition, it can, from a worldly point of view, pose considerable difficulties for your family and friends, and even your employers. You may find it hard to concentrate on the matter which is under discussion; you may become forgetful of ordinary things, even though your memory for the detail of your Catholic interests is disconcertingly exact. In such circumstances it may be helpful to have some suggestions on how to deal with the situation.

There are cases where the nature of the call of God is so clear that it is possible for some very decisive people to determine immediately what they should do. But not everyone receives grace in the same way as St Paul did, in a blinding flash of light, and is able to respond accordingly.

Indeed, the accounts of the conversions which I have mentioned, and my discussions with other converts, suggest that, for a great many, the process of conversion has come very slowly. Of course we must all beware of anything which might be putting God to the test, or which might be a rejection of the grace being offered by Him. But it seems to me that, as part of His great love for each one of us, He actually tailors His grace for us individually. Each one of us then has to decide how best to respond.

There are several possibilities when you begin to be in the situation I have described, or, when, without feeling such strong symptoms, you suspect that something is afoot. The first is to spend as much time as possible in prayer. Many of those who are already Christians are almost certainly doing this, although, in my own case, when looking back, it is surprising how little time I seem to have spent in real personal prayer.

Our Lord himself, in His earthly life, set us a good example. The lives of the saints continue to show the great importance of personal prayer. But paradoxical as it may appear to be, some people who are in the condition I have described, or who in other ways seem to be touched by grace, may find it difficult to pray at all.

My advice to those of you who are in this situation is not to neglect making an effort to pray, but to concentrate on short prayers such as the Lord's Prayer. If you cannot even manage this, or don't yet know it by heart, you might simply say "Lord teach me to pray", or "Lord, help my unbelief". Child-like repetition of something very simple at this stage may be all that is possible. Indeed it may be all that is needed.

By you might also try simple prayers for other members of your family or your friends, who may be having difficulty in coping with you in your new condition. These short prayers may help you to become less self-absorbed. You may also need to pray for strength, to be able to cope with criticism that by becoming more concerned with God, or "religious", as the unsympathetic may call it, you are becoming more "selfish".

Because of their different traditions and differing theology some Christians may have never prayed for those members of their family who are already dead. Even though most Christians have some form of belief in the after-life, and know that the "communion of saints" is a doctrine they confess to believe in the Creed, they do not usually think through its implications. You may find it easier, at least initially, to explain to those who are dead what is on your mind, and pray that *they* understand, than to find the right words to explain your feeling to living members of your family.

It may also be useful to remind yourself that most Europeans have Catholic ancestors. At least some of those in the past can be expected to understand your prayers! Some of you at this stage may even be able to say a shy word of greeting to Mary, the Mother of Our Lord. For if we can be in communion with those who have died, then the marvellous thing is that we can also be in communion with that human being whom God chose to be His mother when He came on earth as a man. It is amazing how difficult talking to Our Lady can be to some, and how easy it can be to others, who are literally amazed that they have never thought of doing it before.

But there will always be a large number of people who will not find prayer of any kind at this stage easy. To them, the idea of prayer is putting the cart before the horse. How can you pray until you know more about what you believe, or whether you believe at all?

And here it is important to remind yourself that while faith, like the other theological virtues, hope and charity, is ultimately a gift from God, the Catholic truths on which it is based, are consistent with human reason. For many it is a great source of consolation that this is so. There are many people who have lived in the past, or are still living now, who are much, much cleverer than most of us ordinary mortals; and yet they have come to be Christian believers. After careful consideration and lifelong reflection, these men and women have come to accept the great Christian truths. And what is more, and this seems to me to provide great insight into God's love for each one of us, He has also made it possible for these truths to be understood by each one of us, however different our levels of intelligence. In other words an important sign that the Catholic Faith is true, is that it can be understood at a number of different levels. A Faith which could only be understood by those who are clever, would not be one for the whole of mankind.

Whether or not you begin with prayer, or follow a more intellectual approach towards belief, it will be essential at some point to acquire some detailed knowledge of what Catholics actually believe, or rather what the Catholic Church teaches. As we shall see, this is not always the same thing.

Fortunately, there is a marvellous little booklet, entitled *A Catechism of Christian Doctrine*, which is approved by the Catholic Archbishops and Bishops of England and Wales. The first edition appeared in 1889. It was then known as "the Penny Catechism" as this was it price at the time. The most recent edition was published by the Catholic Truth Society in 1985. It is generally available in bookshops specialising in Catholic books; it can often also be found on sale at the back of many Catholic cathedrals and churches. It is a work of extraordinary richness. When considered in the light of the benefit it offers for the saving of souls, it represents quite extraordinary value for money, currently at 50 pence!

I would suggest that everyone enquiring about the Catholic Faith should purchase a copy of this little catechism and browse through it. Some of it may seem incredibly simple. You should remember that it is designed to be able to be used for explaining the Faith to everyone. It therefore needs to be clear and precise. Other parts are more complicated, at least if they are read without having understood the earlier parts.

The Catholic Faith is a complete system of belief. Catholics believe that the way it all fits so amazingly together is a proof that it is divinely inspired, and hence true. The catechism seeks to explain the essentials about the relations between God in His three persons, Father, Son and Holy Spirit, about human beings, and their relationship with God, and with one another, and about the nature of the world which God has created. The Catholic Faith does not allow you to put your religious beliefs in one compartment of your life, and your ideas about the nature of the physical world, and about what is right and wrong in human behaviour, in another.

You may at first sight find this rather strange, or even repellent. Many people in contemporary society pick up their ideas about honesty, sexual behaviour, the sanctity of human life, life after death, and other important matters, from those about them, and from their reading of newspapers, modern books, and from discussion with their friends and family. This is not the Catholic way. As a Catholic you may not find it always easy to live in accordance with the teachings of the Faith, but, once instructed, you will know what the teachings *are*, and how each part of them fits together with every other part. You will thus have a secure foundation. It is important to come to terms with this right from the start.

One further point. The emphasis in the catechism is on achieving personal salvation and holiness. Superficially, this may seem rather "selfish". But consider this more deeply. It is only by learning how to save one's own soul and keep it safe, and learning about the nature of God, and building a right relationship with Him as a result of that knowledge, that you will be able to be used by Him to help others, both spiritually and materially. Only then will you be able to play a useful part in building His kingdom.

When you think about it, it is simply common sense. Your part in the redemption of the world is to help others to salvation. In order to play that part, you need to be able to teach others accurately. To be a teacher of anything you must first learn your subject. To teach the Catholic Faith is no exception to this general rule. You cannot ignore the rules of human reason in matters of religion.

Just one further word about the catechism to which I have drawn your attention. In Rome in 1985 the Holy Father, as many Catholics like to call the Pope, presided over a synod of Catholic bishops of the universal Church. This synod decided that a new catechism should be produced for the Church. When this appears, it may differ somewhat in form from the catechism to which I have drawn your attention. In the same way the English and Welsh bishops' catechism is different in form from the catechism produced by the Council of Trent in the 16th century. But the fundamental truths will remain the same, however differently they may be expressed.

Doctrine develops. But just as an oak tree is, in a fundamental sense, contained in the acorn, so all the elements of the Faith as it now appears to us in the teachings of the Church, were at least implicit in the teaching of the early Church. Catholics also believe that, since God became man, and founded a Church to spread His kingdom on earth, He would not allow us to take a fundamentally wrong turning in matters of doctrine, no matter how much human weakness or temptation may lead some of our popes, bishops or priests astray in their personal lives. Since the Church was founded by Our Lord himself, it is reasonable to believe that He would wish to ensure that it did not deviate from the truth.

The Catechism is full of spiritual riches, and has a great deal of majestic beauty in it, as you would expect from something which tells of the things of God. Yet I doubt if many people will be able to absorb all the essentials of Catholic doctrine and life from reading this on their own. Most people will need some sort of commentary. Some of you may think that the right approach at this stage would be to seek personal help from an expert, such as a Catholic priest or well-informed lay person.

For reasons which I will explain, I suggest that it may be better to delay such a course of action for a little longer. Of course, if you have a close Catholic friend, you could ask him or her for help. But there is a risk that those you go to may not be fully capable of explaining to you all the essential points of doctrine, and putting them into simple but unambiguous language, however well-grounded they are in the Faith.

Although, in general, Catholics have traditionally been better taught in their Faith than many from other Christian churches, there is no doubt that the standards of education in the Catholic Faith, like the standards of education generally, are less good than they once were. Regrettably, there is sometimes a gap between practising the Faith, and having the words to tell others about it clearly and precisely. One of the major tasks of every Catholic, as I shall indicate later, is to try to remedy this.

The need for accurate knowledge of the Faith is particularly important when it is a subject, which, like mathematics, is one where you need to understand one point, before you can fully understand the next. Those like me, who missed a few crucial lessons in mathematics, and then found themselves floundering, could have some similar difficulties, This can be the case with the Faith, even though we know that God will always give us sufficient grace to understand, provided we remember to go on asking Him!

The present plans to bring in regular assessment and testing in secular education in England and Wales throughout primary and secondary education, show that this need for a good grounding is once more being accepted and understood. The same detailed step-by-step approach, with clear objectives and a regular review of progress, is probably a good approach also to the Catholic Faith. In practice it may not be easy to find someone to help you in this. For this reason, those who wish to begin to grasp the truths of the Faith in a more informal and personal way, may consider acquiring a commentary at this point.

God has been at work, and there are two comparatively recent ones which are ideally suited to the purpose. For those who prefer a book, there is a marvellous one entitled *We Believe*. Originally this appeared as an anonymous publication. Where you would expect to see the author's name on the cover, the reader is simply informed that the work is "By a Priest". But the writer's cloak of anonymity has now been stripped away, and his modesty uncovered. The author, Monsignor Gilbey, now acknowledges his marvellous gift to the Church. The book is based on a course of instruction given by him to enquirers into the Catholic Faith.

Monsignor Gilbey is a legendary Catholic priest. He was Catholic chaplain at Cambridge University for many years, and now lives in retirement at the Traveller's Club in Pall Mall, London, where he has a tiny private chapel in an old boot room. Over the years, he has had a profound influence on a whole generation of Catholics, both young and old. Many owe their Faith to Monsignor Gilbey in one way or another.

For those who would prefer to listen to a commentary on the catechism, rather then read one, there is an excellent one on tape by Father Hugh Thwaites. These tapes are available from Christus Vincit Productions, PO Box 17, Rainham, Gillingham, Kent ME8 OJU. Father Thwaites is a convert, a former Anglican, and a Jesuit. As well as being extremely learned, Father Hugh has worked for many years with students from overseas and among the immigrant community in Brixton. He is therefore well-practised in putting the Faith across simply and clearly. There are six tapes, and in them he covers the 370 questions in the Catechism. This may sound rather daunting and exhausting— a bit like coping with one of those mammoth plays so beloved by some modern producers, or listening to the whole of Richard Wagner's *The Ring Cycle*. But it is quite easy listening. I once spent much of an Easter holiday gripped by them. I know others who have heard them have found them not only instructive, but have been charmed by Father Hugh's lightness of touch, joy and humour. Many are only eager for more when they come to the end of the six tapes!

Father Hugh has also made tapes on a number of other topics, such as Confession, which are also available from Christus Vincit. Once you have got a good idea of the nature of the Catholic Faith you will want to reflect carefully upon all aspects of it. So some of the other tapes may be helpful.

Nevertheless, you should remember that most of us will never fully understand all aspects of the Faith this side of Heaven. I sometimes find it consoling that even the disciples who were acquainted with God in the person of Our Lord on earth, who saw His miracles, and experienced His resurrection, had to live by Faith after His ascension. I feel sure that many of them had to face spiritual trials, which suggested that their experiences with Our Lord were all a dream, or that somehow they had come to misrepresent what they had seen. But in the end they remained steadfast, and it was through Faith that they managed this. We have to live by the same Faith.

We will be presented with many points about the Catholic Faith in the catechism and the commentaries. Many of us will also, please God, be inspired by some good people we meet, or have met, who are Catholics. But in the end we still need God to give us the grace to recognise that it is the Catholic Church which has been charged with preserving His revelation. The Church has indeed been founded by God

Himself in the person of Our Lord. This is the reason why the great doctrinal system fits together in the wonderful way that it does.

Once you begin to suspect the divine origin of the Catholic Church, and start to recognise that, despite the ups and downs of church history, and the failings of many of its members, including St Peter right at its very beginning, it still retains the essential nature of the God who founded it, you may be ready to think about the next steps.

For many people there will still be many difficulties, cultural and historical, as well as doctrinal, holding them back from actually taking a decisive step towards becoming a Catholic. In Britain, history, as taught in most schools, and in popular folklore, is still biassed against the Catholic Church, even in these ecumenical days. This is perhaps understandable. A continuing theme of much of British history has been the conflict between the Catholic Church and those who wished to change it or destroy it.

When Henry the VIIIth quarrelled with the papacy about his wish to divorce Queen Catherine and marry Anne Boleyn, the dispute at first appeared to be about Church discipline and authority. Henry VIII continued to believe he was a Catholic, long after the breach with the Pope and the rest of the Church. Even so, he certainly showed few signs in later life of practising the Christian virtues. The Protestant ideas which by now had become strong in much of the northern part of continental Europe became firmly established in England under Edward VIth. There was a sincere, but misguided reaction under the Catholic Queen, Mary Tudor, who tried to compel Protestants to keep the Faith by violent persecution.

How much better it would have been if she had been guided by a St Francis de Sales, who brought back to the Church many parts of Switzerland and Eastern

France, by patient love for the people, the goodness of his life, and the courteous way he presented his arguments.

Under Queen Elizabeth it was the Catholics' turn to suffer. The persecution of Catholics increased once the Catholic Faith had been successfully equated with treason by Elizabeth's ministers, following the Armada invasion. It continued under King James, after the Gunpowder Plot was used by his ministers to stir up anti-Catholic feeling. The long period from Elizabethan times up to 1829, during which Catholics had no civil rights and experienced periods of fines, harassment and imprisonment, bears testimony to the long-standing prejudice against Catholics. More recently, the troubles in Ireland, have also helped make many Britons wary of Catholics.

But of course there are other reasons for anti-Catholic prejudice. These derive from historical events outside Britain, and from Protestant propaganda levelled against the Faith. A useful book which can help people understand many of these issues is *Difficulties*. This is a correspondence, in published form, between Sir Arnold Lunn, whose family founded one of the earliest travel agencies, and Ronald Knox, a Catholic priest and a former Anglican clergyman.

This is a genuine exchange of real letters, not a literary device designed for publication. At the beginning of the correspondence Lunn is sceptical, if not actually hostile to the Catholic Church. A year or two after the correspondence ended, Lunn became a Catholic.

The letters are a quite amazing example of a conversion to the Catholic Faith, in which the means of grace is the personal letter. You can almost see grace at work before your eyes, as the letters go back and forth, and the points of dispute and concern arise, and are patiently dealt with. The letters raise many of the issues which have been traditionally regarded as "difficult" for Catholics to explain: the Inquisition, Papal infallibility, indulgences, Popes who have led immoral lives which caused scandal. Part of the charm of the correspondence is the humility and reasonableness with which Father Knox puts his case, and the great courtesy with which Lunn replies.

Taking a Decisive Step Forward

In God's good time there will come a point when you have read a great deal on your own, and you are, I hope, beginning to spend much time in prayer. You know that you are now ready to take a further step. This is in many ways the most important decision of your spiritual journey. Hitherto your interest in the Catholic Church has been largely a private matter, just like any other interest, known perhaps only to some close friends and members of your family. A decision to make some contact with the Catholic Church can be a much more public affair. You will need to be prepared for this.

But before you take this step, some of you may have to face one last assault from the father of lies, as the devil is often called. He may well counsel you against being rash, emphasizing the problems, emotional, sexual, even career difficulties which you could face, if you become a Catholic. He will tell you that you will lose your freedom; that you will have to believe everything that the Pope says.

The devil may encourage you to "understand" the Catholic Church so that you can enjoy its art and music, and its contribution to Civilisation. But he will try to prevent you from formally committing yourself. If he cannot persuade you to drop the whole thing, he may encourage you to stay on its fringes, going to its services occasionally, and drawing some spiritual benefit from it, without actually committing yourself. He will prefer a Catholic collaborator, rather than a true member of the Church, if he cannot keep you away from Christianity entirely. You will need to pray hard for grace to resist this, if his attack takes this form. I can think of a number who have stumbled at this stage.

But having resisted this, and decided to go public about what is on your mind, you will need to prepare your family and close friends. You cannot become a Catholic in isolation. If you feel that your religion is your private affair, you many find this strange. But the Church will not normally accept a secret conversion.

I say "normally", because I know of a case of an elderly lady, who had been editor of a Church of England newspaper during her working life. When she became a Catholic in old age, she asked the Catholic community, through which she was brought to the Church, to keep her conversion secret, in order not to upset her family, and former newspaper colleagues. This was accepted by the priest who received her, although whether it was the best solution is a matter for the theologian.

Once you are learning about the Faith, the representative of the Church to whom you turn for advice, will certainly want you to become a Catholic. He may well ask others to pray for you. This is a task often given to communities of monks or nuns, but lay people may be asked to do this as well. After my reception I often met people whom I hardly knew, who had been praying that the advice on the Faith which I received, would lead to my entry into the Church. Some people may regard this as an intrusion into their privacy at first. But eventually you will, I'm sure, be grateful for it.

You will also need to accept the fact that there is a risk that, once you are receiving instruction, and this will normally be done by a priest, this fact may well become known to others. You could, I suppose, ask him to preserve confidentiality. But that could be like asking him to accept some hinderance in his job of acting as a channel of grace for you.

Obviously, once you have approached a priest you may fear embarrassment. Supposing, having heard more about the Faith, you decide against becoming a Catholic. Would it not be better if the fact that you had taken this step was not generally known? My own view is that, as in so many situations, openness and honesty are the best policy. It is better simply to explain truthfully to your friends and acquaintances what you are doing and why.

I am sure that the best of them will be understanding, if you take them into your confidence in the first place, even if you feel you may be vulnerable. Although this is unlikely to be uppermost in your mind at this stage, it is also better not to involve the Church in something which might be presented as underhand. Naturally, all Catholics will hope that a decision by you *not* to seek admittance to the Church, after a period of enquiry, is only a temporary setback. Their hope will be that you will eventually receive grace another way. But no organisation, let alone God's Church, wants a reluctant recruit.

Of course, some of those reading this book may feel that they do not need much personal help at this stage at all. After all, they may have made a careful study of the books suggested, and perhaps many others as well. They may know the details of the catechism very well. Prayer may have resulted in their having great confidence that they are ready to be received into the Church. Some may even have been ministers in other Christian denominations. Perhaps they have spent their whole lives studying theology.

A few may know that Cardinal Newman himself

spent only a few days being prepared for reception by the priest of the Passionist mission in England, the Blessed Dominic Barbieri. Indeed, it is always possible to be received as a Catholic at short notice on one's deathbed, or in other extreme circumstances: King Charles the Second, the art historian Lord Clarke, and the Labour politician Lord George-Brown, were all received as Catholics at the very ends of their lives.

But I believe that for ordinary people, in good health, the Church is right to insist that enquirers should have a period of formal instruction from a priest. They need the human contact with the Church. The Church is not an abstraction. The disciples brought new converts to meet Our Lord personally. It is important to have the opportunity to talk over the Faith, and to discuss any difficulties with a sympathetic priest. He will also be your first guide on matters of Catholic practice, morals, and the "norms of piety". The latter are the ways by which you are helped to keep close to God in His three persons, to Our Lady, and to the saints who have gone before us.

If you are anything like me, all this will take quite a long time. Indeed, there is a great amount that you will not be able to learn in any period of enquiry, however long. But it is important to get a good grasp of the basics. The last thing you will want to happen is that you are received as a Catholic after an inadequate preparation, and then find it difficult to continue to practice your Faith because of this.

But first you need to decide whom you should ask to tell you more about the Faith. Of course history is full of marvellous stories. Some people simply knocked on the door of the first priest or monastery they came across after they decided to receive instruction. The grace of God did the rest. But there are many of us, even in the midst of the tumultuous surge of emotion which can accompany the decision to seek instruction, who feel they need to be prudent. Prudence is indeed one of the cardinal virtues.

For those who feel, as I did, that God wanted me to make a sound decision, based on the best possible advice and assistance, there are a number of choices. Some of you may have Catholic friends, whom you particularly respect. One possibility would be to seek their advice. Some of these may indeed be able to make good suggestions. But you may be surprised, particularly if they were brought up as Catholics, how little they know about which priest will be keen and able to take people on for instruction. Of course all priests should be able to do this. But there will obviously be advantage in finding a priest who will understand *you*, and the kind of problems which you may have been facing, not only intellectual, but also emotional and personal.

Catholics who are converts themselves may, in some circumstances, be better placed than those brought up as Catholics. They may at least be able to advise you on some of the pitfalls. Some of these may recount how chaotic their own instruction was! On the other hand there are many priests brought up as Catholics, who have developed a deserved reputation for preparing converts for reception. Much depends on the person being instructed and the priest concerned.

If you have no Catholic friends, or are too shy to ask them, you may simply have to make a choice on your own. What are the possibilities? The first, and perhaps the most obvious way is to find out who your local Catholic parish priest is, and consult him. He may be ready to prepare you himself, or he may suggest another priest, who, he considers, may have the right qualities to suit you.

But practical and other considerations may encourage you to consider other options. You may work far from your home, and arrive home late, so that it may not be possible to meet a priest in your home town or village at a reasonable hour in the evening. For one reason or another weekends may be difficult too.

There are other considerations, apart from convenience. It may be prudent to try to ensure that the person who tells you more about the Faith is skilled in the task of instruction, as well as being able to provide you with the answers you need. Of course all Catholic priests should be well - trained, but, being human, they do differ in their talents.

There is another factor to bear in mind. Since 1988, the Catholic Church in England and Wales has brought into effect a scheme which lays down the approach for the Christian initiation of adults into the Church. This sets out how the decree of 1971 of the Universal Church's Congregation for Divine Worship in Rome should be implemented.

Broadly speaking, the approach of the *Rite of Christian Initiation for Adults*, or RCIA as it is known, distinguishes two phases of approaching the Catholic Faith. First there is that of enquiry, sometimes dignified by the name of the precatechumenate; and secondly that of the formal preparation of the unbaptised for admission to the catechumenate of the Church. "Catechumen" is in origin an ancient Greek word which was used by the early Church to describe someone who is learning about the elements of the Christian Faith. What we are considering at this stage is the choice of person to help in the first phase of your enquiry, the precatechumenate.

If you do not go to your local priest at this point, how are you to choose among the other possibilities? I would suggest that you should normally look for another Catholic priest. But you need to be sure that he really is a Catholic priest. This may sound paradoxical. But it could be an important point for those coming to the Catholic Faith from a non-Christian background, or who have had little contact with the organised Christian religion. For someone like this, it could be easy to assume that a High Church Anglican minister, who calls himself Father, and says he is a Catholic, is really a genuine Catholic priest. You might wish to ask such a person if he is a Roman Catholic. Of course the true situation would eventually come to light, but it could be embarrassing.

For this reason it is always worth checking that a priest is in the Catholic Directory for the diocese in which you are in. You can usually find the directory in Catholic bookshops, or in some local libraries. The directory has a lot of other useful information about Catholic societies and religious congregations, and the times of services at churches and monasteries and convents in the diocese. But when you choose someone to give you advice on the Faith, you will not only want him to be a genuine Catholic priest, but also someone who is orthodox in the Faith.

What do I mean by this? I am simply making the point that it is of greatest importance that anyone who gives instruction should really hold and teach "the Catholic Faith that comes to us from the Apostles" as the words of the Holy Mass put it. I would wish you to be taught the whole Catholic Faith in all its completeness and majesty. He should not be someone who conceals from you any elements which seem difficult, or might put you off, because they do not seem to be in keeping with what he understands to be the views of the modern world.

He should himself be someone who is completely faithful to the teachings of the Popes, as the successors of St Peter, as expressed in their encyclicals. He should be loyal, as one says, to what is called the "magisterium" of the Church.

I have no doubt that one of the worst things which can happen to a convert is that he or she is taught the

Faith by someone who seeks to make the whole thing easier and more comfortable, in worldly terms, than it really is; who implies that you will have to make no changes or sacrifices in your life, in order to become a Catholic. That is not the Faith for which the martyrs died, nor the Faith which the saints embraced. The priest who instructs you should not be one who implies that some doctrines or moral obligations are optional.

Of course Catholic priests are just human beings like you and me, although they have received the added grace of the Sacrament of Holy Orders. Many of those who try to make the Catholic Faith less of a challenge undoubtedly believe that they are acting for the best. But anyone who is really thinking of taking the great step of becoming a Catholic, with all that this involves for their relationship with God and other people, will want to do this on the basis of the whole truth of the Faith, and the moral teachings which flow from this. They should not be satisfied with some watered-down version of it.

It really is in no-one's interest that the "hard sayings" of Our Lord, or the spiritual or moral aspects of the Faith, are played down. For let us be clear: the teaching of the Church is very different from the kind of advice you would receive from an "Agony Aunt" in the newspaper, from "professional counselling", from welfare agencies, from a non-Catholic religious minister, or from concerned members of your own family.

But how can you be sure that the priest whom you choose to provide advice will present you with the fullness of the Catholic Faith as it really is, so that you see clearly the divine origin of the whole system of belief as it is unfolded to you.

A wise old priest told me he has two tests to guide him on the completeness of a priest's view of the Faith. The first relates to his attitude to Our Lady, as the Blessed Virgin Mary is generally known to Catholics.

In his view, only really orthodox priests understand her key role in the history of salvation. Without a love and understanding of her it is very easy to blur and misinterpret the key Catholic beliefs relating to Our Lord, the Blessed Trinity and the Church.

The second test, he suggested, relates to a priest's attitude to Pope Paul VIth's encyclical, *Humanæ Vitæ*, *On Human Life*. This deals with such important issues as the nature of the soul, human sexuality and contraception. It is interesting that it was this encyclical, which many Catholics found difficult, which led the writer, Malcolm Muggeridge, to the Catholic Church. For many people, including, regrettably, many Catholics, it is a difficult stumbling block. But a full acceptance of this seems to me an essential prerequisite for someone instructing others in the Catholic Faith. The acceptance of it is a kind of touchstone for being a Catholic in the modern world.

For the values of the encyclical are eternal; they are contrary to so much for which the modern world stands. The encyclical proudly stresses the supreme value of each individual life; the need to be ultimately responsible for one's actions; the value of not sacrificing the weak for the mere convenience of the strong; the importance of the spiritual over the material; the fact that it is never right to do wrong, so that good may prevail. It is a refutation of the utilitarian idea that the greatest good for the greatest number is the right basis for modern ethics.

The encyclical comes with all the authority of the Church, and someone entering the Church has to be ready to accept that authority. We cannot remind ourselves too often that the Church is a divine institution founded by God himself in the person of Our Lord. The Church, despite being composed of sinful humans, when She speaks, speaks with authority. The fact that what She says when She speaks with authority may be difficult to practice, and may not accord with current worldly wisdom, is a powerful sign that Her voice is an authentic one.

It is this test of obedience that those entering the Church will need to recognise, if they are to enjoy the full riches of the Faith. As you go deeper into the Faith, and it is a wonderful lifelong journey I assure you, you will come to see this encyclical as evidence of the Providential hand of God guiding the Church. For the message of the encyclical stands as a sentinel warning us away from many of the twentieth century paths, which beckon us so invitingly to pleasure and superficial "freedom", but which will lead us, as well as others in society, to our ruin.

Of course it will not be a simple matter to carry out such a test of a priest who is to advise you on the Faith. You might well be accused of lack of humility in approaching the Church if you appear to do this blatantly. My advice then would be to keep your eyes and ears open, and ask questions of others before deciding on a priest to instruct you. Better an escape from a false start than inadequate instruction in the Faith.

If you have difficulties, you might approach Catholic religious congregations and organisations with a reputation for firm orthodoxy such as the Oratorians or Opus Dei. The Oratorians have houses in London, Birmingham and Oxford. The Birmingham Oratory was the religious house to which Cardinal Newman belonged during nearly all his life as a Catholic.

Opus Dei is a comparatively new organisation within the Church. It was founded in Spain by Monsignor Escriva in 1928. Some Catholics have been wary of Opus Dei because of the concerted attack on it made by some journalists over the years. Even within the Church, its strong growth, and the loyalty it attracts from its members, appear to have attracted a touch of envy from some Catholics, including some members of older religious congregations. This is a regrettably human reaction: the Cistercians, the Dominicans, the Franciscans and the Jesuits all experienced similar envy and misunderstanding, when they were growing very strongly and spreading their influence widely in times gone by.

The support which the present Holy Father has given Opus Dei, by making it a personal prelature, and the fact that Monsignor Escriva has recently been declared venerable (the first stage on the way to sainthood), should be all the guarantee Catholics need of its orthodoxy, and the value of its work. But in addition a number of British bishops have long given encouragement to Opus Dei, or the Work, as it is familiarly called. If you were able to find a house of Opus Dei nearby where you live or work, one of their priests might be able to help you at the enquiry stage.

Obeying The Voice Of The Shepherd

Once you have taken a decision to commit yourself to discussion with a priest, and have decided to whom you should go for this, you will need to take a number of practical steps. These are of two kinds, those which relate to you personally, and those which relate to your family and friends, and perhaps to those with whom you work. Even before approaching a priest, you should make a personal vow to allow adequate time for the period of enquiry. Our Lord in the gospel mentions the need to make adequate preparations in His parable about getting ready to build a tower (Lk 14: 28-30).

I say this, on the assumption that you are in good health. A different situation applies if you have reason to believe that you have little time to live. For someone in this situation, it may be consoling to know that, even if you die before you actually become a member of the Catholic Church, you may well be baptised into the Church by what is called the baptism of desire. But in circumstances of serious and mortal illness, a word to the priest will ensure that he takes the appropriate steps for the whole process to be shortened. But normally I am sure that it is best to plan on a number of months, rather than weeks, for the process. Many people may well feel that they should allocate a year for all stages.

At the same time you will want to resolve not to allow the existence of a possibly long period of enquiry as an excuse for putting off the final decision. The exact period will need to be decided by the priest and yourself, in the light of each of your commitments, and the stage you have reached in your own self-instruction, and in your prayers. Some bishops lay down a minimum of time for instruction, with provision for exceptions, if a case is made for this.

Here I should say something more about the RCIA programme which the English and Welsh bishops have adopted. The rules are rather different for those who are already baptised Christians of other denominations, and for those who have never been baptised. For the unbaptised, the general assumption is that they will, in due course, enter the catechumenate, if their period of enquiry encourages them to go further.

Once you are formally admitted to the catechumenate, and this is normally marked by a liturgical rite in the church in the Catholic parish in which you live, it is expected that you will eventually become a Catholic. Usually this admission to the catechumenate takes place in Lent. A series of ceremonies follow during which the catechumen confirms his or her willingness to proceed, and draws closer to the life of the Catholic community and to the Faith. Reception into the Church, in which baptism, confirmation and reception of the Blessed Sacrament are given in the same ceremony, usually takes place at Easter.

Normally, the priest who has been helping an unbaptised person during the enquiry stage, will get in touch with the appropriate parish priest, if and when there is mutual agreement that the person should become a catechumen.

For *baptised* Christians of other denominations, there is no provision for formal admission to the catechumenate. But a local parish priest may make some arrangements for joining with the catechumens in some aspects of instruction or liturgical activity, if this seemed appropriate.

Whatever your own situation is in regard to baptism, your period of enquiry is a wonderful opportunity to learn many things about yourself, as well as the Catholic Faith. I was glad that I did not rush mine. You may well learn a great deal of wisdom and common sense from someone with much experience, arising from his care for the souls of others. So use the time well. The priest will have his own ideas about how best to approach your instruction. But do not be afraid to draw up you own list of points you want covering, and any difficulties you have with doctrine or aspects of moral teaching.

I would suggest keeping a diary for the period of your enquiry phase. In this you can record progress and keep a list of points for further study. Many of you will want to be sure to cover such issues as how human free will is to be reconciled with an all-knowing God; pain and suffering, especially of the apparently innocent, like children; praying to Our Lady and the saints, hell and eternal damnation, evolution and the teachings of the Church in regard to the account of creation in Holy Scripture; purgatory, human sexuality and Christian marriage. Undoubtedly many other issues will occur to you, as your discussions continue. The priest will undoubtedly suggest to you a number of additional books which may be helpful, if he judges that you are the sort of person who will profit from this.

It is doubtful that you will find the complete answer to all the major religious issues which have occupied great minds over the centuries. But it is important that you get to know the range of possible answers which the Church gives, and which have enabled men and women like you and me, over the ages, to make the final leap of Faith. But remember that God will always leave you free. He will not compel you to believe. That would be contrary to allowing you free-will. He will never overwhelm you with arguments which bulldoze their way through your human reason. He has great respect for your individuality. That is why continuous prayer is vital throughout your period of enquiry.

While you are preparing yourself to take the formal step of enquiry, there will be a great need to prepare your family, relations and friends, for your changing circumstance. For those who are already a member of another Christian church, there is also the question of the approach you should take towards those members of the clergy who presently have care of you.

In my view, a very important duty is to your family. This is consistent with the great stress laid on the family in Catholic teaching. If possible, I suggest that you tell them in good time before you begin your regular meetings with a priest. If you have previously managed to discuss the issues openly, your actual decision to take this step may not come as a shock. For some extraordinary lucky ones, more than one member of a family may have reached the same stage of grace, so that you are able to decide to seek instruction at the same time. Malcolm and Kitty Muggeridge were received together. But those who don't find this possible may like to be consoled by the fact that Frances Chesterton was received as a Catholic a number of years after GK Chesterton, her husband.

In matters of religion, it is difficult to decide whether to press on alone, or to wait for a spouse or close friend in the hope that the other will also be given the grace you have received. If you do decide on delay in the interests of the other, you need to be careful that this does not become an excuse for procrastination. There is a sin against the Holy Spirit which is "resisting the known truth" (Question 326 of the Catechism). Unnecessary delay, in the face of grace being offered to you by God, can result in harm. You need to be careful that you are not playing games with Him. Remember that each human soul has his or her unique relationship with Him, which must be cherished. Your task may be to show the way to another, then seek grace for him or her through your prayers after your reception.

Whether you are to pursue your enquiries alone, or with another member of your family, you will need to explain the position to others. Take great care in choosing a good time for this, and that it does not come out in an offhand or haphazard way. What you are doing is one of the most important things in your life. Others should be made aware of its importance. It will usually be as well to make a special arrangement, and to have enough time to explain the matter, even to someone who is very close to you. This may seem rather a formal thing to do. But formality is really only a sign of the importance we attach to the thing we are being formal about.

Obviously you will want to pray for the success of this discussion before it occurs. Each one of us will have our own way of tackling the matter. This will depend on our own situation, and the relationship we have with the other. But there are some general points which it may be helpful to consider.

I would seek to avoid any kind of argument. If you have previously been a member of another Christian denomination, and the other belongs to this, avoid being drawn into controversy. Avoid doctrinal discussion. You may believe that you know quite a lot as a result of your reading. But it would be quite exceptional if you were able to put this into any kind of adequate language, which will convince another of the truths of the Faith. It may be worth remembering that you will not yet have the additional grace from the Holy Spirit. You will only receive this if you persevere to your reception into the Church, and receive confirmation.

In any case, few people are converted by argument. It will be the quality of your new life which will be the most effective source of encouragement to others. The emphasis should be not on what you already know, but on your humility and willingness to learn about the Faith. If you can manage this, I would try to convey to others something of the beauty and joy of the Faith which is attracting you, without suggesting that you are being swept along by a tide of emotion.

If true, you may wish to stress the continuity of your spiritual development. For many, receiving further information about the Catholic Faith, will simply be another stage in a long process of spiritual development. This was true in my case. Be generous. Give due credit to those who have nurtured you in the religion or denomination of your birth or upbringing. Often they can be considered part of the chain of grace too. Above all avoid saying too much, especially if you judge that it may be in danger of creating controversy. One of the Desert Fathers of the early Church, St Arsenius, said: "I have often been sorry for having spoken, but never for having held my tongue". Try to be moderate and loving to the other who may be feeling abandoned. Make clear that you do not know everything. You are receiving instruction in order to know more.

What should you say about the eventual outcome, and how long it will take? Indicate truthfully that you don't know what the outcome will be, or exactly how long it might take. But you should not leave any doubt that, provided you receive the gift of Faith at the end of the period of enquiry, you are prepared to be received as a Catholic. It is important that you do not give the impression that you are learning about the Catholic Faith as if you were simply taking an evening class in a foreign language, or in car maintenance, or musical appreciation, to see whether it appeals to you. That is not the right approach to sacred things!

Some members of your family may also want you to spend the period before you begin a regular programme of discussion, or while you are engaged in this, in reading other books. They may suggest books which disagree with the Catholic Faith, for the sake of "balance". They may even suggest that you talk with some "expert".

It seems to me better to decline these suggestions. But in doing so, you should make clear that you are not doing this out of any unwillingness to consider all the evidence, or a failure to see all sides of the question. But rather that the time for doing this has passed. Normally you will be able to point out that you have already done a great deal of reading in the period up to your formal decision to learn more from a member of the Church. The next step is rather to understand more fully what the Catholic Church teaches, test the way it deals with important issues, and understand your own responses, rather than to launch yourself afresh into controversy.

However, you should make clear that you are very ready to raise any controversial issues with the person giving you instruction. Your family or friends may feel rather powerless to help you, if you are unwilling to listen to their suggestions for further reading, or for meetings with experts. One way of giving them a part to play, if they have some religion, is to suggest that they pray regularly for you.

Many potential converts discover that the greatest fear of those closest to them is that their conversion will mean a radical personal change, and that the relationship with the other will change also.

Of course becoming a Catholic ought to make people struggle to be sinless, and hence behave better towards their fellow human beings. With God's grace, which you will continue to need to seek all your life, there is no doubt that you will make progress. But, being fallen creatures that we are, this will not always be apparent to outsiders. All the faults of character you have accumulated during your life so far will not disappear suddenly. Indeed, you may find that, while some of your most trivial will disappear, other more serious ones will boil up and threaten to overwhelm you. It is important that you are warned in advance that the devil will not leave you alone, just because you are considering becoming a Catholic.

Moreover your family and friends may have got used to your little ways, your small acts of selfishness, your witty gossip, tinged with exaggeration, unkindness towards others, humorous sexual allusions, and jokes about what is sacred. They may fear that any change will destroy the essential "you" that they know, and have come to love. You may in their view be in danger of becoming less "fun" to be with. They may worry that there will be whole topics of discussion where you will no longer be "free" to say and think what you like. You may even be accused of risking "losing your sense of humour".

Experience shows that this will not happen, although some of the things you previously found funny will seem less so. But other aspects of life will become funnier! It seems to me no accident that some of this century's most comic writers, J B Morton, who wrote under the name of "Beachcomber", G K Chesterton, Hilaire Belloc, Evelyn Waugh, Malcolm Muggeridge, Muriel Spark were, or are, Catholics. Indeed you may eventually come to the view it is non-Catholic, or at least non-Christian writers, who are often gloomy and without a sense of fun!

But this will not be easy to get across to your family and friends. They will rightly see what you are doing as something "serious". They will at first confuse this with doing something gloomy. The heavy hand of Puritanism still hangs over the British idea of religion!

They may also think that you will become more predictable in what you say and think; and that you will be always expected to put forward the doctrinal and social teaching of the Church. Of course this will be true in matters of Faith and morals. But there will be vast areas of thought and belief where a Catholic is just as free as anyone else to develop his or her own ideas. Moreover, even where vital issues of doctrine and moral teaching are concerned, you will want to use your common sense in deciding how to express the viewpoint of the Church. Many aspects of the Faith are better lived, than put forward in a controversial manner.

But your family and friends will need reassurance on all of this. They will need to recognise that there is no contradiction between being "fun" and being "pious". This may take a little time to establish. And of course, initially, while you are under instruction, the serious side of you may well, very naturally, be uppermost.

You will want to talk all this over with your family and friends. You will not, of course, be able to predict exactly what you will be like after you have been received. There will undoubtedly be some changes. But, with the help of God's grace, most of these can be expected to be for the better. Nor will you be able to be sure in advance what God will ask of you. All you will be able to say is that, on the basis of what is known about other converts throughout history, you will be "recognizably the same". But perhaps they will be faced with a more "enhanced" you! Of course you will hope that your family and friends will exercise some consideration towards you in your tender new state! But the onus will be on *you* to set a good example, and hence breakdown any mistrust of others.

Telling Those Who are Spiritually Responsible for You

A major issue for some is what to say to members of the clergy of other Christian denominations or other religions who have some responsibility for you. There are a number of possibilities. Some people wait till they have completed, or nearly completed, their period of formal enquiry, before telling their local clergyman or minister. But it seems to me fairer, and more open, to do this in a personal interview before you start this process. A high standard of courtesy towards others is desirable. What you do will, after all, reflect not only on you, but also on the Catholic Church of which you may become a member. It is to be devoutly hoped that your decision to receive formal advice about the Faith is not against the background of personal antipathy with your own clergy. Of course it is possible that some aspects of your present church may not be to your liking. You may have doctrinal concerns. But you need to remind yourself constantly, if this is indeed the case, that it was on this Christian foundation that you have received the grace to go further and seek instruction.

Some of you will have already been baptised, and for many this baptism will be accepted as valid by the Catholic Church. As you will know from the Catechism (Q. 228) all that is needed for baptism is that water has been poured on your head at the same time as these words are said: I baptise you in the name of the Father, and of the Son, and of the Holy Spirit. A proper record of this is clearly desirable, and some proof may actually be needed. From your baptism you will have already received a great deal of grace for your life as a Christian up to this point. What you are considering doing is to deepen your Christian Faith, and bring it to completion. This is the aspect to stress at your meeting with your minister. You will want to make clear the gratitude you feel for all that you have so far received from the church to which you have both belonged. You should also seek to ensure that your personal relations do not suffer as a result of any step you may take. I would stress the special importance of praying for this.

You will also need to be specially sensitive to the fact that, whatever you may say, he or she may still feel a sense of having failed you. There is a risk that the minister may take the view that your action is in some ways a criticism of all that he or she stands for and believes. Avoiding controversial discussion, as I suggested you should do with family and friends, is undoubtedly the best policy. At the same time you should take care to avoid saying anything which might imply that the truth is anything other than you now see it to be. You don't want to confirm someone in a mistaken view!

There is also the question of deciding what you should do about religious practice while you are learning about the Faith. You will probably want to spend a good deal of time in prayer in Catholic churches, if they are reasonably accessible. You may begin to feel something of the particular presence of Our Lord where the Blessed Sacrament is reserved. Although you will not be allowed to receive Him until you have completed the necessary steps for entry into the Church (and you should strongly resist any temptation to do this prematurely and illicitly), you may well find it helpful to attend Holy Mass, and familiarise yourself with the order of the service. Potential converts may find going to Benediction, the special Catholic service of devotion to the Blessed Sacrament, particularly helpful and strengthening.

If you are already a Christian, what are you to do about attending services in your own denomination while you are under instruction? Some people find this difficult to do. It can appear to be rather insincere. Some may find it hard to go on as if nothing was happening, especially if some members of the congregation know what they are doing. But if you normally attend services with your spouse, or the rest of your family, or a close friend, it seems to me better to continue to do so. This may well help to keep these ties together at a difficult time.

Should you continue to receive communion in your present church, if it has this as part of its custom? Here the right thing must be to consult your conscience, and discuss it with your minister. Again those close to you may feel abandoned, if you change your practice abruptly. You should also discuss the matter with the Catholic priest who is instructing you. Pray a lot about the matter as well. Remember that one of the most painful things that will happen, if and when you are received as a Catholic, is that you, and those members of your family and friends who are not Catholics, will no longer be able to receive communion together. This reinforces the need for prayer and keeping close to Our Lord, and for his guidance on how best to help your family.

Those who have been practising other religious faiths will have similar issues to resolve, and much prayer will be needed. You too will also want to take advice from the Catholic priest who is advising you, since there are important issues of family solidarity and friendship, which need to be protected. Those who are unbaptised and have no religious background of any kind may have a simpler situation to deal with at this time.

Formal Enquiry

Most people who seek advice on the Faith have to fit this in with their ordinary daily lives. For those who have a full time job this will mean seeing a priest, or whoever is to give you instruction, in the evenings, at weekends, or during a holiday period. Sessions once or twice a week will probably be what will be suggested. The amount of instruction will depend very much on yourself, and the judgement of the priest. Try to spend a little time in prayer before you attend each session. Ask God to enable you to use the time wisely, and to give you an increase of Faith. It is marvellous if there is a Catholic chapel or church nearby. You will want to make sure that you do whatever reading or spiritual preparation which is asked of you as carefully and conscientiously as possible. Aim for a spirit of perfection right from the start. Make a point of being punctual. But don't be concerned if the priest himself is late. Remember that he may have many other things to do, apart from offering instruction. Learn to be charitable at the beginning of your great endeavour.

While I was an enquirer, the priest who was advising me was called away to give the last rites of the Church to a dying man in hospital. Remember that there are others souls, apart from yours, who may need what only the Church can provide. Use any time of waiting in prayer, or in assembling your thoughts better, and in going over in your mind the points on which you need explanation or reassurance.

You will, of course, want to spend a good deal of your leisure between sessions in thinking about all the issues of faith and morals on which you will need guidance. But remember that you cannot expect to know everything about the Faith from a period of formal enquiry. If you enter the Church, you will, I am sure, meet many converts of forty or fifty years standing who will tell that their Faith is more and more of a blessing every year, and that they are still learning. Of course, you will know intellectually that this must be the case, since what the Catholic Church teaches is God's truth. But it will be reassuring to have it confirmed by different people in all walks of life.

During the enquiry stage, make sure that you have a full discussion about the Church's teaching on moral questions, especially sexual morality. If you are married this will affect your spouse, and will call for much patient discussion, and perhaps considerable changes in the way you behave. You will need to learn something about the Catholic attitude to birth control, and what is acceptable to the Church.

Many who are not Catholics are coming to see the virtues of natural rather than artificial methods of birth control. The patience and respect for each other which the latter requires can be an enormous aid to a lasting love which is based on unselfishness. It is a splendid rebuff to the worldly view which holds that human beings, like animals, not only should not, but in practice cannot, control their sexual desires. This view is held by many who recognise that in other aspects of behaviour it is possible, or desirable, to control the body. For instance, they can accept some restraint on their appetite for food, or to obtain mastery of the body for sport, or to promote physical fitness. The whole history of family life and celibacy, in both the Eastern and Western tradition of the

Catholic Church, shows how mistaken the generally-accepted twentieth century view, that you should never seek to master your sexual desires, really is.

This may also be the time when you and your spouse ought to think positively about the arguments for having more children. This book is not a polemical one. But it may be worth reflecting, when confronted by arguments in favour of tiny families, that the whole Christian position is based on a belief in the ultimate providence of God. The prescription in Holy Scripture to be fruitful and multiply makes sense. The older you get, the more you will see the consequences of rejecting this view.

For a society which is not generous in the matter of having children is really rejecting the theological virtue of hope in the future. It is also likely to be a society where the virtue of charity to others is weak. For those in the prime of life who are married, but are not bringing up children, will tend to develop habits of selfishness. And this is likely to be reflected also in their attitude to the care of their elderly parents or other relations. Again Holy Scripture and God's Commandments remind us of the requirement to look after them, but a lifetime of selfishness will make it more difficult to rise to this challenge.

Small families inevitably find it more onerous to make adequate provision for elderly parents. Indeed we are increasingly seeing how a materialistic society, without a firm belief in God, and in the value of each human soul, begins with contraception and abortion, then risks moving on to allowing euthanasia for the vulnerable elderly and the seriously disabled. As individuals and society become more self-centred, the next step on from this could be to require euthanasia, for some categories of persons, as a public duty.

As in questions of doctrine, I do therefore commend to you the orthodox Catholic position on such moral issues. I am sure that you will come to see it as an integral part of the Faith in its richness and entirety. You wont always, I'm afraid, always get the full teaching from every Catholic priest. As I have suggested earlier, there are some priests who in a laudable wish to be understanding of human weaknesses, leave those who come to them in error about the truth. Yet if you follow the Church's full teaching, you will be amazed how much additional grace you will receive. And that which seemed so difficult at first will become easier and more rewarding, and a source of great inner strength to a family.

Once you have cleared your mind on these issues, and the doctrinal points which need explanation and understanding, you and the priest will need to reach an understanding on the next step. I hope that by now God's grace will have enabled you to reach a decision. The rest of this book presupposes that this has indeed been the case. If not, I thank you for allowing me to take you so far along your particular spiritual journey. If you are not received, I pray that God will find some other way to offer you an increase of His grace.

Gateway at Spello
near Assisi

CHAPTER TWO

PASSING THROUGH THE DOOR

HAVING decided to be received into the Church, you will now wish to consider with your adviser the next step. If you are unbaptised, and your instruction has been from a priest of the parish in which you live, he is very likely to suggest that you now enter the catechumenate. You will then follow the rites prescribed for catechumens in the RCIA, culminating in your full reception into the Church at Easter.

If the RCIA is well-organised in the parish, this may be a good chance to get to know other potential Catholics, and some existing members of the parish who may be involved in helping with the introduction of catechumens to Catholic life. If you are unbaptised and being instructed outside the parish, the priest who is preparing you may well now suggest that your reception should take place in your parish. This is really a matter on which he and the parish priest will need to reach agreement. The normal arrangement would be for you to enter the catechumenate at an appropriate time, and follow the pattern laid down by the bishops: admission to the state of catechumen, formal enrolment, which ratifies your readiness for full initiation into the Church, and finally reception through baptism, confirmation and reception of the Blessed Sacrament. The main benefit from this process is that you will receive liturgical support for your gradual commitment, as you draw closer to the Church.

As I have indicated, this is not an option for those who have already been properly baptised within another Christian denomination. There is much more flexibility for them as to timing, and to some extent, as to the nature of the ceremony. Again the question of whether you should be received in the parish or not will need to be discussed between the person who has been advising you, and the parish priest, if the latter has not been preparing you.

With this greater flexibility, you will also want to consider whether your family and friends would like, or feel they ought to attend the ceremony of your reception. To the extent that you are able to influence its timing, you should also consider the supernatural aspect. The priest preparing you may have ideas on this. It may be possible to fix your reception for a day when a saint to which you are particularly attracted is commemorated. This is like inviting another close friend to the celebrations. Try to remember that your reception will be a cause for joy in heaven.

Your reception could be the occasion to show special regard to Our Lady. If you have not understood this already, you will find her a particular help once you are a Catholic. Choosing one of the days special to her for your reception can get you off to a very good start in the Faith. As you will have learned, every normal Saturday is a time to remember her especially. Then there are her major feast days: the Annunciation on the 25th of March, the Visitation on the 31st of May, the Assumption on the 15th of August, and the Immaculate Conception on the 8th of December. The entire month of May is specially dedicated to her.

Having fixed on a date and a time, the priest who is to receive someone already baptised within another Christian denomination will need to give your name to his bishop. This is where you will need evidence of your baptism. The priest will also have to indicate how much instruction you have had. Depending on the circumstances, you may have one additional thing to do. If you have already been baptised, and are being prepared individually, you will need to make arrangements to make a general confession to a priest. The priest who is preparing you may arrange to do this himself, or he may organise another priest for this. He may, however, leave this for you to arrange.

For a general confession, you need to examine your whole life, to the best of your ability, and consider it against the laws of God and the Church, as you have learned them in the catechism. Once you have made this examination of your life, you will be in a position to confess where you have broken these laws, show sorrow for what you have done, and receive absolution, that is God's forgiveness for them.

It all sounds thoroughly alarming, and indeed it is. It is one of the most momentous things which anyone can do in his or her life. What you are doing is putting into words, for the benefit of Our Lord, all the dark secrets of your soul from your birth. Of course, because He is God, He knows everything that you have done already. But in order to change for the better you need to acknowledge your sins yourself. One thing, however, which should help cheer you up is that it was for this purpose that God became man: to bring us to repentance, and set us on the right road. And in the person of Our Lord He underwent Crucifixion to free us from the death to which our sins, unrecognised and unrepented, will inevitably lead us. So, if after baptism we have broken his laws, it is vital that we get back into a proper relationship with Him.

I hope that you will come to see, as I have done, that confession, or the sacrament of reconciliation as it is sometimes called nowadays, is one of the great wonders and blessings of Catholic life. At first you may think that the whole idea of confessing your sins to a priest is difficult.

You may ask yourself why you should not confess directly to God. Of course this is what we are doing during confession. But the Catholic Church believes that an important means of doing this, which is of particular benefit to us, is through the sacrament of penance. Penance was instituted by Our Lord as a means by which the sins we commit after baptism are forgiven, and we receive strength to avoid sin for the time to come. Our Lord said to His disciples, who were the first priests of His Church: "If you forgive the sins of any, they are forgiven; if you retain the sins of any they are retained."(Jn 20:21). St James says: "Therefore confess your sins to one another and pray for one another, that you may be healed." (Jas 5:16).

In forgiving our sins, the priest is acting in the person of Our Lord. The priest simply acts as the channel for God's grace. And just as we all, however weak and sinful we may be, are able to act as the channel of God's grace for bringing others to Our Lord and His Church, so the priest, duly ordained by a bishop, the successor of those originally appointed by Our Lord, is able to act as a channel of grace for us in confession.

Even if we were unaware of the sacrament's divine origin, our own reason should enable us to see its value to us. For confessing to another encourages the important virtue of humility. And humility is a precondition for all the other Christian virtues. The fact that we are encouraged to give precise details of our occasions of sin to another, to find the words to do this, and that we may have to go on confessing the same sin very often, should help us remain humble. Moreover, the regular practice of examination of our conscience, against the standards of God's law, and the requirement to find out the true facts about ourselves, will help ensure that we do not deceive ourselves, and pretend that we are doing well, when we are not. Pretending to be good when we are not is true hardness of heart, which Our Lord condemned when He was here on earth.

And at confession we have the priceless benefit of a priest's counsel. There is something essentially brotherly and sisterly about confession. Of course Our Lord is our brother, since He lived on earth like us, and experienced all our human weaknesses, yet without sin. This should be of great comfort to us. But it is surely a sign of His mercy that He has entrusted the sacrament to His priests. For although the priest forgives us in the person of Christ, there is something very consoling to know that the priest too has been struggling against sin, and will be in turn confessing his own sins to another.

Indeed confessing our sins to another, and encouraging each other in the struggle towards sanctity, will increase our sense of brotherhood and sisterhood, and mutual support. I am sure you will come to see confession as one of the greatest gifts which God has given to His people.

In order to get yourself ready for a general confession you will need some guidance on how you should approach this. Of course, if you consider the Ten Commandments and the Commandments of the Church, about which you will have learned when studying the catechism and during your instruction, you will have a good idea of where you have gone astray. But a good guide to confession is valuable.

A useful one for examining your conscience is to be found in the Catholic Truth Society's A *Simple Prayer*

Book. For the more traditionally-minded, there is also a good section in Bishop Challoner's *Garden of the Soul*. A particularly fine modern one, in a handy format which can be kept in a breast pocket or handbag is *To Prepare for Confession*, published by Tamezin Publications of 2 Chelsea Embankment London SW3. This singles out the five elements of a good confession:

1. examination of conscience;
2. sorrow for sins;
3. the intention of not committing sins again;
4. the accusation of our sins;
5. satisfaction or penance.

The booklet then takes you through the ways in which you ought to examine your conscience in regard to your life, to see to what extent you have been guilty of breaking the commandments of God or His Church. If you are anything like me, when you read through this you will be rightly appalled at what you have done, and what you have failed to do. But cheer up. Remember always that the whole purpose for which God became man and suffered as He did, was to save you from your sins. So you have good grounds for hope. Of course you will, naturally, feel quite miserable to think what a horrible life you have lived up to now, in so many different ways.

Although you normally do not take notes with you to confession, it may be useful to prepare a list when you are preparing for your general confession. Of course you will want to ensure that this list is kept away from the sight of others! You should also seek to avoid any kind of perverse sense of pride in the number and range of your sins. Here it may be useful to remember that sin is very often simply a failure to do what is good. When seen through the eyes of God I am sure that many of our sins seem largely squalid affairs of weakness and inadequacy. Even so some of us will have at times done things which are particularly evil or devilish.

We often choose the easy, instinctive, animal way, rather than that which seems more difficult and which, in our heart of hearts we know to be the more noble. Having listed your sins, and got yourself in a frame of mind in which you are genuinely sorry for them, and having resolved to try not to commit them again, you will be ready to make your first confession.

You will find some good advice on what you should do, and on what exactly takes place at confession on page 17 of the Catholic Truth Society's *A Simple Prayer Book*. You will want to ask Our Lord and Our Lady, your patron saint, and other saints for whom you feel a special veneration, not forgetting your guardian angel (a lovely friend who has been watching over you since birth), to help you make a good sincere confession. There is a useful prayer for use before confession in *A Simple Prayer Book*, which you might say just before actually beginning your confession.

There are now two ways of receiving individual confession. One way is to do this kneeling down before a priest or sitting with him in a room in the presbytery (Catholic priests live in presbyteries, presbyterian ministers live in manses; Anglican ministers live in vicarages, rectories or parsonages; it is all rather confusing!). Sometimes, a Catholic priest will arrange confessions in a room attached to a church.

Alternatively, you can make your confession, more anonymously, in a confessional in a church. A confessional is usually a small box-like construction, normally free standing and of wood, which you see in most old Catholic Churches. The penitent, as he or she is called, kneels on one side of a screen or grill, and the priest is on the other. There is often little, if any, light in the confessional, apart from the light of the church. A tiny light above the confessional usually indicates if a priest is there and is hearing confessions.

This type of confessional can have a slightly intimidating effect on a newcomer to the Church. It is so essentially Catholic. It symbolises in a particularly striking way the difference between the Catholic Church, which requires individual confession to God, through the assistance of a priest acting in the person of Our Lord, and other Christian denominations and religions, which either favour corporate confession, or an individual approach to God without human assistance.

As I have explained, the priest is acting in the person of Our Lord in the sacrament of penance. On each occasion of confession he makes a judgement about the nature of our sins, our sorrow for them, and our intention to do better. We are then forgiven, or given absolution, as the technical term for this is. Because of this requirement for confession with a judgement which applies to us individually, we always need to follow up any general *corporate* absolution, which we receive in a group from a priest or bishop, by going to confession by ourself in the normal way.

Box confessionals were introduced originally because of the Church's sensitivity to the idea of women confessing publicly to male priests. Such a confessional preserves a certain anonymity, protects a woman's dignity, guarding her and the priest from the risk that this encounter might in any way be compromising.

Nowadays many men prefer to confess in confessionals too, even though there is a school of thought among some Catholic men, that failing to confess face-to-face to the priest is slightly unmanly. Such men hold that a straightforward uncomplicated facing up to your failings, and confessing them to a priest man-to-man is the better way.

Nevertheless, for new converts, confessing in a

confessional in a big cathedral, can seem like a guarantee of anonymity. This can, at least initially, be welcome and reassuring. Eventually you will come to realise that an experienced priest will have heard so many confessions of frightful sins, crimes and weaknesses, and that the confidentiality of the confessional is absolute, that there is no greater embarrassment in confessing face-to-face, even though one's sorrow for one's sins, and regret at failure to do better, remains as grievous as ever.

There is one further point worth making. Nowadays some priests, in order to encourage people to feel less inhibited about confession, have sought to make this as informal as possible. Obviously, anything which makes it easy for persons to be reconciled to God is to be welcomed. There are marvellous stories of Catholic priests hearing the confessions of strangers while travelling next to them on æroplanes or buses. But there can be a danger that, with too much informality, the penitent, and even the priest himself, may confuse an informal chat, and the provision of advice about personal problems, with the sacred sacrament of penance which Our Lord instituted.

A talk with a priest may be of enormous general value, and I will later say something about the desirability of all Catholics having spiritual directors. But the distinction between this and confession must not be blurred. All the formal elements which I indicated earlier must be there at a confession. Without them, we will not have made a good confession. Above all a confession is not to be confused with the advice which friends or professional counsellors or social workers provide.

Of course making a general confession affects everyone differently. But do not be surprised if confessing the sins of a your whole life results in some tears. It certainly did in my case. The amazing joy of being fully reconciled with God, once all the elements of the sacrament have been completed, is a wondrous thing. As I indicated above, after your confession the priest will give you an appropriate penance. This will often be merely to say a short prayer. To some converts it seems extraordinary that after what seems to you a long and very sinful life, when measured against the commandments of God and His Church, that you are only required to do something so simple.

At some periods of the Church's history, penances were much harsher. But the Church, in Her loving wisdom, now favours less onerous penances. This should encourage us all to go more frequently to this wonderful sacrament. We should also try to carry out the particular penance we have been given as soon as practicable. It can be a good idea to kneel before the Blessed Sacrament in the church or chapel where you have made your confession, so as to carry out your penance immediately. Although it is usually a small thing, you will want to carry this out with as much love and gratitude as you can manage. In a way you are like a child who gives his parents some tiny token of his or her love. The little gift cannot be compared with the large presents that are given by mother and father. But the devotion behind the gift can be very heartfelt, as the child's so often is.

And remember there is also nothing to stop you imposing on yourself some additional act of piety or love for Our Lord. to show your gratitude. Indeed this is a good habit to acquire from the start.

Admission to the Catholic Church

Now you are all set for your reception into the Church. Either you are following the route of the catechumen, or, as a baptised Christian, individual arrangements are being made for your reception, either on your own, or with others. In the latter case, the priest who is actually to receive you should by now have done the necessary paper work. You yourself will have decided whom to invite to the ceremony from among your family and friends.

This can be quite tricky. There may well be some who will be reluctant to see you become a Catholic. Nevertheless, I believe it is much better to offer them an invitation to attend. There is no knowing how the Holy Spirit may work, even if the effects are not immediately apparent. Close friends and family will probably be glad they have been asked, even if some of them decide not to attend themselves, because they are still out of sympathy with what you are about to do.

Whatever the ceremony being used, you will want to make sure that you are completely familiar with what you yourself will need to do. In particular you will want to be able to genuflect correctly, and to make the two different signs of the cross.

A genuflection is an act of adoration to the real presence of God who is really present in the Blessed Sacrament. It is a demonstration of our Faith. It is made when the Blessed Sacrament is reserved in the tabernacle in a church. You should assume that this is the case in a Catholic church unless you know otherwise. A red light in the sanctuary is usually a sign that this is so. On entering a church you either genuflect immediately, or before you go into your seat. You should do the same when leaving the church, either genuflecting as you leave your place, or before you leave the church. You also genuflect to the cross when it is venerated on Good Friday, and to the Blessed Sacrament when it passes you in a procession. Always remember that Our Lord is truly and mysteriously present in the Blessed Sacrament. So you are doing no more than reverencing Him who suffered and died for you.

Some of you may want to know how to genuflect correctly. First stand upright facing Jesus Christ Our Lord in the Blessed Sacrament, to Whom the genuflection is to be made. Unless you are holding something in your hands, your right hand should be placed on the left side of your chest. More ceremoniously the two hands can be clasped together on your chest. Many Catholics don't bother about how they place their hands, but it is worth trying to follow correct form. Then without bending the body, touch the ground with your right knee at exactly the place where your right foot was. You should rise again after a brief pause. You will notice that some Catholics don't always follow this quite correctly. But it is worth trying to get it right by doing a little practice at home!

Now the ordinary sign of the cross. This is made in the following way. Place the palm of your left hand flat on your chest with your fingers extended. Then hold your right hand out in front of you, raise it and touch your forehead. You then touch your right hand at a point on your chest below the left hand, then touch your left shoulder and your right shoulder in turn.

Before the priest reads the Gospel he and members of the congregation make a different sign of the cross. With your left hand on your chest as before when making the other sign of the cross, you use the thumb of your right hand to make a tiny cross on your forehead, on your lips, and on your chest above your left hand.

For catechumens there will have been a fairly careful preparation for the full rite of baptism, confirmation and the reception of the Blessed Sacrament. The parish priest will normally have been given authority by the bishop to administer confirmation for this particular rite. What follows below is particularly addressed to those already baptised in other traditions, where the arrangements are less clear-cut.

The reception of those already baptised will usually

take place during a celebration of the Holy Mass. You will want to familiarise yourself with the service, and discuss with the priest who is to receive you what form it will take. Ask the priest for a copy of the text of the rite to be used, so that you can study it. You ought to be sure that you know the text of the Creed you will be asked to say (or sing!-protest if you can't!) by heart. For those with a sense of history and some linguistic skill, or a good memory, I suggest that you might also seek to learn it in Latin as well. Sometimes the Latin text is used when a person is received. If there is a choice, some people may like to request this, in order to emphasise the link with tradition.

Another point worth considering is offering a gift to some appropriate religious charity on your reception. There is, of course, no reason why a catechumen should not do this as well. Discuss this with the priest beforehand, or with a Catholic friend. Most people will want to ensure that this offering is a particularly generous one, to match the grace you have received. You will also need a sponsor for your entry into the Church. Those requiring baptism will also need at least one godparent. If you are lucky enough to have a good Catholic friend, he or she may be willing to take on either of these roles. Otherwise the priest himself may be able to suggest someone particularly suitable for you. Your sponsor or godparent will be charged with the task of settling you in to the Church, and looking after you in your early days as a Catholic. If you are as lucky as I was, they will do all kinds of things of spiritual significance. It is good to have someone to turn to for practical questions as well. Of course you will also begin to rely on Our Lord and His Mother, and your guardian angel, who you will begin to realise has been looking after you since your birth.

General practical advice at the time of reception

No doubt the priest will have some useful ideas on what books you should acquire for your new life as a Catholic. As a minimum I suggest that you purchase *A Simple Prayer Book*, if you have not already done so. This gives the text of the Mass in English, and of many Catholic prayers and devotions. The Latin text of some parts of the Mass is also included, although not the full text.

If you are at all traditionally-minded, you may wish to have a fuller version of the Order of the Mass in Latin with the English alongside. There is an inexpensive little booklet entitled *The Order of the Mass in Latin and English*, which is widely available. Some entire Catholic services in parts of Britain, particularly in the bigger cities, are in Latin, except for the readings and homily, which is the normal Catholic term for the sermon. Even where the Mass is mostly said or sung in English, some of the great prayers or hymns are in Latin, even if the rest of the service is not. To prepare yourself for this, it can be a good idea to familiarise yourself with the Latin text alongside the English version. This is possible in the booklets to which I have referred.

Normally, where the Mass is in Latin, it is generally the same form of service which you will experience in English. Many outside and inside the Church confuse this with the Tridentine form of the Mass which was also in Latin. For many years after the Vatican II Council of the Church, which began in 1962, the Tridentine form of the Mass was not lawful. But some years ago, the present Holy Father issued what is called an "indult". This was a formal decision which permitted the Old Mass, as it is sometimes called, to be said or sung in certain circumstances, provided the Bishop gives his approval. In 1988 the Holy Father relaxed the conditions for celebrating the Old Mass still further. Bishops were encouraged to make this available where groups of Catholics requested this.

I suggest that you should try to become familiar with the Holy Mass in Latin, both in its new, and in its Tridentine form. Don't be put off by language difficulties. Remember that most of your forbears coped with this. Indeed there was much advantage for a universal church in having the service in one language throughout the world. Using Latin can also help some of us acquire the sense of awe in the face of the enormous mystery which is being acted out before us. Some feeling for the service in Latin, and the great Catholic prayers which have been used by the Church for centuries, will help us experience the full richness of the Catholic tradition.

One point to note if you come from the Anglican Church, is that Catholics, by and large, seem to operate with less books than an Anglican is used to. Many Catholics nowadays do not bring their own missals to Holy Mass. Often those attending are given a practical, but rather tatty-looking, two-sided broadsheet called a missalet. This contains the text of the Mass for the day, including the various readings. This is certainly less confusing than having to find your way around the Anglican Alternative Service book. But its most fervent defenders would not, I am sure, defend its æsthetic charm, or its mistakes and misprints.

I am sure that in due course it is sensible for converts to have a daily missal of their own. These are usually quite expensive, so I would urge you to take your time, and do some fairly extensive market research. They are bulky books. You will want something which is dignified and well bound, because regular use will mean that it will get quite a battering, no matter how careful you are with it. One with a slip cover is a good idea.

An excellent one is the *Daily Roman Missal* which has all the readings in one volume. It is distributed by Sceptre Limited, London. It contains all the prayers for Holy Mass, together with the text of many other prayers and devotions in English and Latin.

A rather confusing, and to some people, a rather tiresome point, is the pronunciation of the word generally used for the rite of Holy Communion. You will find that some Catholics pronounce "Mass" to rhyme with "vase", or "ma" or "pa". Others, and these are more numerous, pronounce it to rhyme with "lass". By and large the pronunciation with a long "a" is more old-fashioned, and some converts prefer it for that reason. One suspects that a slight touch of snobbery has crept into religion in these British distinctions of pronunciation.

You may also find a little volume like Cecilia Bevan's *A Book of Catholic Prayers* useful. It gives the text of a lot of traditional Catholic prayers in English and Latin. It can be obtained from her bookseller son, John Bevan, at St Francis, Great Doward near Ross-on-Wye in Hereford and Worcester. Another spiritual standby, which I have mentioned already, is *Garden of the Soul* by the 18th century bishop, Richard Challoner. This valuable treasure of English Catholic spirituality is an inexhaustible source of joy and comfort. Since it has not been reprinted recently you could also ask John Bevan to look out for a second-hand copy for you. He specialises in old and out-of-print Catholic books.

Even before you are received I would also urge you to purchase a rosary. One of the great joys of Catholic spirituality is getting closer to Our Lady. The rosary is her special devotion. There is a little bit of explanation about it in *A Simple Prayer Book*; and there is also a range of booklets about it available in Catholic bookshops. One of the little booklets for children can be very helpful. They can encourage us to have the right child-like approach to begin with. But since you will have many other things on your mind in the period up to your reception, it may be sufficient just to buy a rosary and keep it in your pocket or handbag, just to get accustomed to having it with you. You will spend the rest of your life, I hope and pray, learning to pray and understand the rosary, at all levels of simplicity and sophistication.

There are many different ways of praying the rosary. These are variations on the basics you will learn in the booklets I have suggested you look for. You will also probably develop your own personal way, and then learn a number of other ways from friends. But however you pray it in detail, the rosary is always a wonderful way of understanding and keeping the Catholic Faith. The fifteen mysteries which tell of the major incidents in the life of Our Lord and Our Lady, five joyful, five sorrowful, and five glorious, are a splendid affirmation of the key elements of orthodox belief. There are few better ways of reminding ourselves of all that God has done for us.

You are now ready to enter the Catholic Church, or as ready as ever one is. You have made sure that your family and friends understand what you are doing and why. You have invited those who would like to be present to join in the joyful occasion. You might even consider arranging a celebration afterwards, perhaps asking the priest who receives you to attend. It may not be possible to have everyone to your celebration if you are received at a parish Mass, especially if your reception takes place at a large church on one of the great feasts of the Church. This may well be the case if you have been a catechumen. But unless you are very shy, I would suggest that some kind of celebration will be in order, to mark the significance of the occasion. Ever after it will be one of the great occasions of your life, and you will want to remember the anniversary in a special way each year.

Once all this has been done, the rest will usually be carried forward by the grace of God, with the help of your prayers and those of your friends. Those of a heroic cast of mind and plenty of stamina might consider a vigil of prayer the night before they become a Catholic.

You will normally receive the Holy Eucharist at the rite which is used for your entry into the Church. If you have already been baptised in another Christian church, you do not need to wait until your confirmation by a bishop to receive communion. Unless special arrangements have been made for the priest to administer confirmation at your reception, confirmation may well take place sometime later.

It may be that on the occasion of your entry into the Church you will receive the Holy Eucharist under both kinds, the Precious Body and the Precious Blood. As you will have learned, Catholics have, for many centuries, normally only received the Precious Body of Our Lord in Holy Communion. This is all that is necessary for a complete reception of the Sacrament. This is because the whole of Christ, Body, Soul and Divinity, is present under the different consecrated species. In other words Our Lord Jesus Christ cannot be divided. Receiving the Precious Blood from the chalice is normally limited to the priest and any other priests celebrating with him, and those assisting him at the altar, although some parishes now offer the Precious Blood to the entire congregation at Holy Mass, either regularly, or on special feast days. Some Catholics regard this as an unnecessary break with tradition, and only receive under one kind, even when the Precious Blood is offered. And they are perfectly free to do so.

Reception of the Blessed Sacrament is one of the greatest and most solemn things which can happen to us ordinary men and women in this life. The fact that we are encouraged to receive Our Lord in this Sacrament frequently, might, unless we are careful, result in our losing our sense of wonder and appreciation. For this reason it is particularly important that this should be done as reverently as possible.

Traditionally reception of the Sacred Host was on the tongue from the hand of the priest. There is an aptness about receiving Our Lord in this way; it has childlike simplicity, and to me it seems instinctively the right way for the soul to be fed. Of course this should encourage the recipient to ensure that their mouth and tongue are in an even better state than when they visit the doctor or dentist! A minimum fast of one hour before receiving communion is enjoined on us. Some believe that we ought to avoid food for longer if we can.

But reception on the hand is now also permitted. In some parishes this is widespread, even encouraged by some priests, although they are instructed not to position their hand in such a way as to discourage reception on the tongue. You are perfectly free to choose either way of receiving Our Lord in communion. Of course the hand of the recipient should also always be spotlessly clean; great care should be taken to avoid any particles of the Sacred Host from falling to the ground, or otherwise being "lost".

Some converts are rather shocked by the fact that in most Catholic churches nowadays the sacrament is received standing from the priest or his assistants in the centre aisle of the church. I must say that I prefer to receive kneeling, and I treasure those churches where this is the custom. The best practice is when there is a server who holds a communion plate under your chin when your receiving on the tongue, in order to be absolutely sure any fragments of the Sacred Host are caught.

One final point. You may, I hope, receive some

suitable pious presents at your reception. These will undoubtedly be very much treasured. Don't be surprised if some simple objects or books of devotion delight you as much as those which previously you might have regarded as in better artistic taste!

After Reception

Many new converts feel an indescribable joy after their entry into the Church. This can last for days, sometimes weeks or months. For these happy ones it feels as if God has wanted to give the new member of the Church an extraordinary personal sign of His grace. This can be off-putting to family and colleagues at work, unless they are prepared for it. They may well find you frequently in a distracted state. It may be quite difficult to get you to concentrate on mere earthly matters. Making appointments, getting decisions out of you, may not be easy. You may need to take conscious efforts to counteract this, reminding yourself of your duty to your neighbour, when all you want to think about is God, His holy humanity in Our Lord, and about Our Lady, and your favourite saints!

But don't be concerned if you don't feel like this. It may be that Our Lord has other ways of offering you His grace, which will be revealed later on. Perhaps He knows you are made of sterner stuff, and do not need this great joy now. This may be being reserved for later. Many of the famous converts have missed out on this great joy, so if you don't feel especially exalted, you are in good company. Some converts even feel rather frightened at the thought of the new responsibilities they have taken on.

Whatever your state, you will want to settle into the routine of ordinary life within the Church as quickly as possible. You will also want to try to start off as well as you can. This normally means endeavouring to instil some greater self-discipline into your life. Order and routine are a splendid thing to offer up to Our Lord, especially if you have in the past found these qualities rather difficult to attain. It is sometimes a good idea to remember that you are simply reflecting the order which God has built into His creation.

You will, by obligation, but with great pride and joy, attend Holy Mass every Sunday and on Holydays of Obligation. You will also become aware that the Church, in Her wisdom, has also enabled Catholics to fulfil their Sunday obligation by hearing Mass on Saturday evening. This can be particularly helpful if you are travelling on Sunday, or have to do shift work on that day. However, you should only attend Mass on Saturday, rather than on Sunday, when you have reasons of real necessity, not simply convenience.

You will also want to make extra effort to attend additional Masses during the week as well. You should choose days for this not only on the basis of convenience, and when you feel devout, but also plan to attend on days which have a special meaning to you in the life of Our Lord, Our Blessed Lady and the saints. There are other days when you may wish to go to Holy Mass, which are special to you or your family: birthdays, anniversaries of the deaths of relations and friends; days of historical or religious significance. A good diary which includes an extensive list of saints, to which you can add days of significance to yourself, is most useful.

Remember that you can also ask a priest to say Holy Mass for an intention of your choosing, say for one of your relations or friends, or someone who has recently died, and whose soul you wish to see in heaven. If he has not already agreed to say a Mass for a special intention on that particular day and time, you are normally expected to make a small monetary contribution for this. The Mass will then be a stipendiary Mass. Remember that priests receive no salary: all they receive is expenses. So this is in part a way in which we can carry out our duty to support our pastors, which you will recall is one of the Church's commandments.

It is a good thing for a new convert to learn something of the other services of the Church, such as Solemn Vespers and Benediction. If you live in a large town or city, it may be easier to find such services than in rural areas, or small country towns. But many small churches offer these services at special seasons of the year, even if they don't offer them regularly. Do seek them out. There are still some churches where there is magnificent liturgy and music particularly worthy of the grandeur of the Faith we profess.

Conversion can also be a good opportunity to set a new pattern of praying regularly for your family and friends. You can always seek special graces for them. You may sometimes think that as God is all-loving He will do whatever is needed for another, provided he or she is ready to respond to His grace. But the Church teaches us, and many of us also have instinctive sense that this is true, that God especially delights in our co-operation in His work of salvation, and in our readiness to act as channels for His grace. Set aside some time for this every day if you can.

With regard to Holy Mass, remember that your obligation is to hear it only on Sundays and Holydays of Obligation. You should only receive Holy Communion when you are in a state of grace. This means that you are not conscious of having committed mortal sin since your last confession. If you have, you need to confess all your mortal sins, and receive absolution before receiving Our Lord in the Blessed Sacrament.

If you are to get to grips with your weaknesses, and make progress spiritually, and grow in sanctity, as you will wish to do, you will also find it of enormous benefit to make a regular confession of your venial, or less serious, sins. In this way you will benefit from the particular grace offered in the sacrament of penance.

Frequent confession of your venial sins is a good way of preserving humility. It helps you to focus your attention on how inadequate your response as a Christian is, when it is compared with the pattern set by the saints. Although this may sound dispiriting, it can be greatly consoling. For an honest examination of conscience, followed by confession and absolution, can be a marvellous source of strength, inner peace, and grace.

You should try to set a regular pattern in your churchgoing as soon as you can, choosing if you can a time of Holy Mass in your parish which is suitable for you. There is usually a Parish Mass with music, and now quite often considerable lay participation in the readings and prayers, and sometimes in the distribution of the Blessed Sacrament. For some people this communal involvement is very welcome. For others it can get in the way of their devotion to God. In many parishes there is also another Mass, often earlier in the day, which is quieter and more reflective. This may suit some people better at first, as being more devotional.

I would counsel all new converts to root their Catholic life firmly in the parish. Of course the Church has always defended the right of individuals to attend Holy Mass wherever they wish. And you may well want to attend other churches occasionally. Indeed you will want to pray and attend Holy Mass in churches near your place of work as well. But it is a good idea to make a whole-hearted commitment to your own parish, its priest, and any assistant priests, if you are lucky enough to have these. Of course there may be circumstances where this is difficult. You may also find the services unappealing, with some aspects which do not suit your spiritual or æsthetic sense. You may even be irritated by the manner or content of the parish priest's homily.

It is as well that you are warned of the possibility of this in advance.

If this happens to you, I would urge you to struggle hard to overcome your feelings. Your growth in self-discipline, which is one thing which your conversion should help you with, will be much aided by such a struggle.

Rather than complain to others and unsettle them, or become secretly resentful, you should try to offer up to Our Lord any dry or uncomfortable feelings, as a special personal sacrifice for His sake. Remember that, whatever the inadequacies of the presentation of the liturgy for Holy Mass, and the particular human quirks which are incorporated into it when it is offered up by a particular priest, it is still the Sacrifice of Calvary. It is Our Lord who is on the altar and in the Tabernacle.

One thing you can do, for your part, is to encourage the priest to keep this reality fresh in his mind by your own reverence and devotion. Priests, for all their wonderful vocation, and the grace and commitment needed to sustain this, are only human. They may need reassuring about their essential role in the liturgy. Some priests have taken it on themselves, or have been encouraged to behave like laymen, in order to become "closer to the people". The method used to get closer to their flock, which is indeed a laudable objective, is not always appropriate, and can, in fact make them less effective as priests.

Signs of a weakened sense of the magnificent treasure of the priesthood are a priest's readiness to abandon clerical dress when "off duty". Priests may even have been told that this will help them to be better received where their presence might otherwise cause some embarrassment.

In my view, priests should be continually encouraged to see that being visibly a priest on all occasions is a most powerful demonstration of the reality of our

Faith, and its power to overcome the world. To appear apologetic about it, whether in church or out of it, can be damaging to the dignity of Our Lord. An important part of lay peoples' duty is to encourage their priests to retain awe for the dignity of what they have become, priests forever after the order of Melchizedek.

A priest who wears clerical dress all the time is readily identifiable to everyone, and is thus a potential source of spiritual help for any person who may need to be reconciled with God. How many souls throughout history have been saved by a chance encounter with a priest! The priest who received me had a marvellous story of hearing a man's confession, and giving him absolution, while they were alone together in a lift between the ground floor and the top of a multi-storey building. This was only possible because he was clearly recognizable for what he was, a priest of Our Lord's Church.

Our reverence for the dignity of the priesthood, and our encouragement to priests to preserve a sense of their special worth, needs to be combined with considerable personal friendliness and kindness to them as human beings. There can be much loneliness if parishioners set their priests apart in the ivory tower of their presbytery. To strike the right balance can take a little time for a convert to achieve. It needs to be worked at and prayed about. You will also want to do what you can to fit your priest into your family circle and personal life. But you need to be sensitive to his vocation, his vows of celibacy, and the requirements of his own rule of life (eg his obligation to say his breviary each day).

It is worth encouraging the priests of your parish to make full use of their special power to provide blessings. Invite a parish priest to bless a new house when you move into it, or to bless the completion of a new extension, or a new development of a part of your garden. At key moments of your life you may wish to ask for a special blessing from him, and receive this kneeling before him. Seek to cultivate a natural, unaffected spirit of piety in regard to your parish priest.

But what if you find yourself completely out of sympathy with the way your parish priest conducts himself, or performs the liturgy? You have tried, perhaps for several years, to offer up your feelings to Our Lord. You have tried, unsuccessfully, to encourage the priest to have a greater sense of his priestly dignity. But you feel you have made no progress. In a spirit of fraternal correction you should then try to discuss the matter with him, praying beforehand that you may find the right sensitive words for this. This is never easy, either for you or him. But he has a right to know how you feel.

Some priests, although I hope not many, may tell you that because what they are doing is satisfactory to many others in their congregation, there is no need to make any change to suit the few who express concern. But in many cases you can expect a reasonable hearing. This may clear the air, and help you both to go forward together with some renewed understanding of each other's position.

The problem of a priest's personality and style in the liturgy was one which was perhaps less of a problem with the old Tridentine form of the Mass, which was universal in the West before the Second Vatican Council. The form of the liturgy was laid down in such detail, with the emphasis on creating a timeless act in which an individual priest had little scope to "personalise" the service. This may perhaps have made it easier for him to be seen as acting in the person of Christ, rather than as human being leading corporate worship of the divine.

If at all possible, you should seek to attend your parish church regularly. This is undoubtedly the best way to build a satisfactory framework for your spiritual life, even if everything is not always done there which is perfectly to your liking.

There are only two reasons for not attending Mass regularly at your parish church. The first is if you come to believe that your parish priest is not teaching the Catholic Faith. This can happen. The influence of Hans Kung, who previously taught as a Catholic, but whose writings have now been officially condemned by the Church, still persists, as does that of some other "modernist" theologians, who have abandoned the essence of the Faith, as it has been handed down since Pentecost. In trying to "bring Catholicism up to date", they have fallen into various errors. Of course Our Lord predicted this, and the history of the Church has confirmed His prophesy. But it is still a shock when it occurs.

Even a new convert should never be afraid to raise points of doctrine with his parish priest. If the answer does not seem in accordance with the catechism, he or she should not be afraid to say so. If the explanation still seems unsatisfactory you should never hesitate to raise the matter with your bishop. Of course, it is courteous to tell your parish priest that you intend to do this before you do so. The Faith is too precious to allow it to be compromised through lack of vigilance.

For a source of sound doctrine laypeople should try to keep up with the Pope's encyclicals. This will help keep them well-informed on important doctrinal and devotional issues. In an extreme situation, if you are not satisfied that what you are being taught is the Faith, you might, after much prayer, and discussion with a spiritual adviser, withdraw from the parish and seek to attend elsewhere.

The second reason for not attending Mass in your parish relates to the liturgy. It can happen that the services offered in your parish are so alien, undignified or bizarre, that it is quite impossible for you to focus your attention on Our Lord, and the Holy Sacrifice of the Mass. As I have indicated above, I would encourage you to make every endeavour to have the situation improved by discussion with the priest and other parishioners. Even if you appear to be making little headway I would still urge you to persist and persist, with much prayer, offering up your difficulties and making sure that your attitude is not based on prejudice.

But if the services still have the same effect after a long time, and the priest appears not to be concerned about this, then, and only then, should you consider attending Mass in another parish. You will want to inform the priest's bishop of the action you are taking, and why.

What I have written above may suggest that a new convert may well have difficulties. But this is likely to happen rarely, so I would expect most converts to find the main framework of their religious life within their parish.

But once you are settled in, there is no reason at all why you should not go outside your parish for special functions, weekday services, or some of the feasts of the church. This can add richness to your spiritual life, and help you develop an understanding of the Catholicity of the Church and its tradition. Indeed I would urge all new converts to make a special effort to attend some of the splendid and solemn services at the great cathedrals, abbeys, convents or churches, which have great musical and liturgical traditions.

It is becoming more common again for churches to use the musical settings for Holy Mass and other services which were composed by the great masters of the past. Many of these are now frequently heard in the concert hall. But how much better to hear them in the setting for which they were written, and where those attending have an understanding of what the composer's true intentions were. There is something slightly bogus about a lot of modern day materialists and pagans applauding a "performance" of some piece of sacred music in a concert hall, as if it were a secular work. It is often said that it is good to introduce those outside the church to the richness of its artistic traditions, in the hope that some hint of the glory for Whom it was intended, might reach others. Paintings of Our Lord and Our Lady in an art gallery can sometimes act in this way.

But I am not sure that, in the case of music composed for the liturgy, the advantages for the Church are not outweighed by the disadvantages. For there is a serious risk that familiarity with a work, performed away from the spiritual purpose for which it was intended, can encourage viewing spiritual things only against criteria of taste, or beauty, or sensation.

Confirmation

It can come as a complete surprise to some converts who have previously been "confirmed" within another Christian tradition, that new converts to the Catholic Church will need to be confirmed again. This can seem particularly odd, even incomprehensible, to some converts and their families. As we have seen, becoming a Catholic can be considered simply as a development of an existing Christian faith, and not a fundamental change. Many Catholic priests will emphasise this continuity during instruction. And there are obviously some basic common elements. The Creed is the most important of these, although nowadays some of its basic tenets are questioned by some contemporary theologians of other Christian churches.

Confirmation, however, highlights the fact that

the churches are still divided, however much goodwill and Christian charity there are between them. The other churches' separation from the One Holy Catholic Church, which Our Lord founded, cannot be ignored as though it never happened. Thus, for example, the Catholic Church still does not recognise Anglican Orders of church ministry. The force of the Papal Encyclical, *Apostolicæ Curæ*, which sets aside Anglican orders as null and void, still applies, despite all the ecumenical conversations and dialogues which have taken place over the years since it was first issued in 1896. The reasons for this are set out in the encyclical. They relate to the continuity of the Apostolic succession, and to the nature of the Anglican ordination service itself.

Of course it is important to realise that this does not mean that no grace at all was conveyed by one's previous "confirmation" within another Christian church. But it is not the kind of sanctifying grace of the Holy Spirit which Our Lord has given to the Holy Catholic Church to bestow.

Those who have previously been "confirmed" will be able to judge the difference. I believe that you are likely to be aware of the additional power which you will acquire from this. It will help you with particular weaknesses of character, such as lack of self-discipline. Do not be surprised if some weaknesses seem easier to overcome. But don't imagine that they will disappear entirely! At a later stage they may return and give you a shock. The devil won't let you go so easily!

As I have already indicated, those who have been through the catechumenate will usually be confirmed at their reception. The parish priest will usually have been given authority to do this. But others may need to be confirmed by a Catholic bishop at a separate ceremony, Adult confirmation in this case can be a fairly big affair. It frequently takes place in the Cathedral of the Diocese. Where the bishop has co-adjutors or assistant bishops, these others often take it in turns to perform the ceremony.

It is customary to choose a new name for confirmation as it is at our baptism. Some priests forget to mention this in good time before the ceremony. I have known occasions where there has been a rapid search for a new name just before the service! You will want to consider your confirmation name with some care. You might consider the name of a saint whose life particularly appeals to you, or of one who, in the past, has had some connection with you. It could be the saint of a church where you have received special grace, whom you would like to honour and seek to befriend. You could also choose the name of the priest who received you, or the bishop who confirmed you, or that of some other person who has played a significant part in the development of your Faith. For preference, I would always choose a name which has a particular resonance in Christian tradition, especially if your original first name has only secular connotations.

You will also need a sponsor for your confirmation. It could be the same person who sponsored you at your reception. Or you might choose another Catholic friend. If you are stuck about whom to ask, the priest who received you may be able to suggest someone suitable. The sponsor's duty is to be beside you when you go up to receive the gift of the Holy Spirit, and to watch over your life as a Catholic afterwards. Your sponsor can be one of the greatest sources of grace for you. Mine certainly has been.

You will want to make similar preparations of prayer before your confirmation as you did before your reception. Make sure you make a good confession before the ceremony. Some devotional reading about the coming of Holy Spirit is likely to be helpful. A good way of beginning well would be to read the Acts of the

Apostles right through from start to finish. This is also known as the Gospel of the Holy Spirit.

You may be surprised after the ceremony that an adult does not automatically receive a certificate of confirmation. I have never heard a convincing reason for this. I suppose the assumption is that, since the adult knows that he or she has been confirmed, and so does God, a mere paper record is not essential. It may date from penal days when it was actually dangerous to be a Catholic. Nowadays a record of your confirmation will be kept at the Cathedral where you were confirmed, but you may have to ask specifically for a piece of paper for yourself. You may need to do this if you later wish to receive the Sacraments of Holy Matrimony or Holy Orders. I would encourage you to get your own record. Subsequent historians of your family may be interested to know when someone in the family returned to the Old Religion, as the Catholic Church is often called in Britain.

CHAPTER THREE

IN THE UPPER ROOM

ONCE you are confirmed you are a full member of the Church which Our Lord Jesus Christ founded at Pentecost, with all its privileges and obligations. Some of you may be conscious of a certain added power. In particular you may find you have received some increased facility for explaining the Faith to others. Of course all Christians have this duty. The old-fashioned word is to proselytise, which was occasionally used about Catholics with some horror. You will later want to learn much more about the Faith in order to do this better. But the grace of confirmation can give you the confidence to begin to confess your Faith, and make a stab at explaining its main points to your friends and relations.

But again do not worry if you feel little of this immediately after your confirmation. Our Lord may have other ways and times in which He will make special use of you. Perhaps He may wish to strengthen you through His sacraments first.

Whatever your feelings after your confirmation, it is important, if you have not yet done so, to start developing your own rule of life. The Church lays down a minimum standard of things which you should do. The basic commandments of the Church are set out in paragraphs 228 to 248 of A *Catechism of Christian Doctrine*. They are:

> to keep the Sundays and Holy Days of Obligation holy, by hearing Mass and resting from servile works;
>
> to go to confession at least once a year;
>
> to receive the Blessed Sacrament at least once a year, and that at Easter or thereabouts;
>
> to contribute to the support of our pastors;
>
> not to marry within certain degrees of kindred.

These are all vital, and you will want to take special care to observe this basic minimum. Resting from servile work on Sundays is not particularly well understood or observed in the busy times we live in. I have usually taken this to mean not doing extra work as part of your paid employment on this day. This does not, of course, apply to those whom society needs to work on that day, for example, doctors, nurses and firemen. I am rather of the view that the rest of us ought also to restrict the amount of work we do around the house and garden, in order to give more time to prayer and spiritual reading.

We should certainly not expect others in the family to spend a large part of their time in household chores, to the exclusion of opportunities to devote themselves to spiritual matters. There is no doubt that it is better for us if we allocate a major part of our Sunday to this, and recreation. At the same time we should not shirk things around the house which really have to be done, especially if someone else in the household might have to do them instead!

But most of us will want to do more than the bare minimum laid down in the Church's commandments to express our love for our Lord, and for the grace we have received. The Catechism has a framework for a Christian rule of life (Qs. 333-354). This indicates what our approach to life as a Christian should be.

Questions 355-370 give some more detailed suggestions for what you might actually do from the time you wake in the morning until you go to bed at night. In particular it recommends beginning the day with a morning offering of one's life to God, some private prayer, and a meditation on a spiritual subject, particularly the life of Our Lord. It suggests that we say grace at meals, and counsels us on what we should do if we feel tempted by sin, or actually commit sin. There is also sound advice on trying to keep a sense of the presence of God during the day. We are urged to attend Holy Mass on weekdays as often as we can. There is a useful suggestion on how we should react to setbacks or illness. And finally the catechism advises us to conclude the day with prayers before we go to bed.

All this is most practical and valuable. The only thing I suggest which might be added is that you examine your conscience every day to see how you are getting on spiritually. Provided you do this honestly, this will help you make progress. And you should also retain your humility when you realise each day how far you have to go.

The marvellous thing about the Catholic Church is the wide range of means which it offers for enlivening us spiritually, and keeping us on the better path. Although the standards the Church sets for us cannot be other than those set for us by Our Lord, it is truly marvellous the wide variety of ways, to suit all our temperaments, which in Her wisdom, She provides for us.

For there is not only Holy Communion, which those from other Christian churches will be aware of, and the other special services of the Church such as Benediction, the Stations of the Cross, and the corporate praying of the rosary. But there is also the great sacrament of penance, or confession, which is such a good means of helping us make progress, and of getting on top of sin and weakness.

And then there is the tradition of spiritual direction. Of course many non-Christians have, what in current language is often called a "guru", or teacher, from whom they seek spiritual or moral advice. And most human beings have friends or relations to whom they go to talk in times of trouble. There are also, of course a whole range of secular "counsellors" or psychiatrists. What the Church has to offer is something particularly precious, a tradition of spiritual advice which has been developed over the centuries, on which individual Christians may draw for their spiritual benefit and comfort.

It is important for those entering the Church to distinguish between spiritual direction and confession, or the sacrament of penance. The sacrament of penance is the means by which an individual is reconciled to God after he or she has committed sin. All of us sin, in one way or another, a great deal of the time through weakness. Even the most holy people have faults which they will be struggling to get rid of. In order to keep the tendency to sin under control, I would suggest that new Catholics should go to confession as frequently as they can.

How frequent this is depends, of course, on one's personal circumstances, and how easy it is to reach a priest. But I believe that most of us should try to get to confession at least once a month, or every six weeks.

This is much more frequent than the minimum laid down by the Church, but less frequent than many lay people, who are seriously seeking to make spiritual progress, aim at these days. I believe it is important to establish an achievable rule of life in this regard early on, and stick to it. It could be a mistake to be too ambitious initially, and then have to confess in the confessional your failure to live up to your earlier resolution! On the other hand, a new convert is not likely to want to set an unambitious target.

You will receive some form of spiritual guidance from the priest when you go to confession. If you go to your parish priest for this sacrament, and you get to know him well, you might ask him to take you on for spiritual direction as well.

But the Church has always recognised that individual souls benefit best from advice on spiritual matters from those who have some understanding of their temperament and character, and have a basic human sympathy with them. However fine your parish priest may be as a priest, he may not be the right spiritual director for you. There are some great spiritual directors who can help a large range of individuals with widely different interests and levels of intellectual understanding. But these are rare. Normally you and your potential spiritual director will realise fairly quickly if the chemistry is right.

A spiritual director will be the person who will guide you on a rule of life for yourself, and help you keep it when you have embarked on it. One of the first rules of spiritual life is to have regular contact with your spiritual director, say about once a month.

But why should you have a spiritual director at all? Would not it be better to stand on your own two feet, draw up your own rule of life and stick to it? There are two main reasons why such a view may be misconceived. First, as a convert you will want to have access to the vast treasure of spiritual wisdom which has been in the Church's care since Our Lord founded His Church. A good spiritual director will have a background in this experience. He will encourage you to develop a balanced regime. He will keep you away from taking on too much, which can result in a sense of failure and depression, if you fail to persist.

He will also encourage you to pursue holiness and perfection in a way which is within your powers at the stage you are at. He will encourage you in your disappointments, console you in your sadness, and help you use your disappointments and inadequacies for the benefit of yourself and others. He will know how to help you to pray better to God, and get closer to Our Lord, Our Lady, your guardian angel, and the saints.

Confiding your failures in spiritual matters, which are for a Christian the most important things in life, is a rather marvellous way of achieving true humility, which I have previously emphasised. This is not at all the same thing as lack of confidence. Indeed it is only by a fundamental understanding of your weaknesses, and the reassurance that God still loves you and wants you to succeed, that realistic self-confidence can be achieved. A good spiritual director will help you pick yourself up, and press on when you are down, and suggest the weapons you need to tackle the enemy who will be attacking you through your weaknesses.

But if you wish to look beyond your parish where should you turn? Of course there is no need for a spiritual director to be a priest. Some unordained members of religious congregations agree to act as spiritual directors. There are even some lay people, women as well as men, with a gift for spiritual direction.

As with choosing someone to tell you more about the Faith, one of the most important preconditions for a good spiritual director is a deep knowledge of it. Directors should also have a well-developed spiritual life themselves, and a commitment to the pursuit of personal holiness. Of course it is also necessary for him or her to have special qualities of human understanding. Your spiritual director ought also to be receiving spiritual direction. This is normally the case with a Catholic spiritual director. This also helps to reinforce the sense that both of you are struggling together.

As I have indicated, there needs to be the potential for understanding between people and their spiritual director. This does not mean the kind of sympathy you find in many friendships. Some friends can be squeamish about telling you the truth. You don't want that at all. Spiritual direction is not the same as friendship. The person under direction needs to feel in some sense in subordination. As I have suggested above, humility is one of the most important virtues which spiritual direction can help you acquire; it is unlikely to be promoted with the kind of egalitarianism which characterises many friendships. In my view it is no bad thing to be slightly in awe of one's spiritual director. This should help you to take direction seriously.

If you decide you have to go outside your parish for a spiritual director where should you look? I have already mentioned that some members of religious congregations have traditionally offered themselves as spiritual directors. The Catholic Directory for your diocese may indicate that there is a monastery, convent or religious house which is not too far distant from where you work or live. Enquiries of Catholic friends may suggest some possibilities.

Some study of Catholic publications may also offer some leads. A careful examination of the writings published by different congregations may give some clues as to the approach which their members might take in spiritual direction. Opus Dei could be a possible source from which to seek spiritual direction. This is one of the specialities of its priests.

Some Possibilities for your Rule of Life

Your spiritual director will have some ideas which you will wish to consider for your rule of life. The grace of God will undoubtedly prompt you to conceive others for yourself. Nevertheless it may be helpful for you to have some ideas before you, which others, down the ages, have found to be of help to them and their families to grow in holiness.

First it is important to build up a good sense of the liturgical year. God, in His providence, has given us a Faith which relates to a series of historical events in the life of Our Lord on earth. Our religion has also been much enriched by the individual lives of the saints and martyrs. By marking the passage of time, days, weeks, months, and years, in relation to these events, the Church has provided us with a marvellous reminder of the truths of our Faith, and an aid to our devotion. The Church has set a minimum framework of hearing Holy Mass on Sundays and on Holydays of Obligation. But someone seriously seeking to make progress in the spiritual life will want to use the other great opportunities which the Church offers for devotion throughout the year.

To begin, let us consider Christmas. This really starts with the spiritual preparation of Advent some weeks before. Advent, when we use it properly, will help us experience the full richness of Christmastide. What a thrilling progress this season makes as it passes by: from Christmas Eve through Christmas Day itself, then on to St Stephen's Day, the Feast of the Holy Innocents, the feast of St Thomas of Canterbury, our great English martyr, to the Solemnity of Mary, Mother of God, on New Year's Day. And finally, still within the twelve days of Christmas, the triumphant Epiphany of Our Lord, when He was revealed to the Wise Men as the Saviour of the World.

What a poor mean thing is Christmas in the secular world, compared with the vision and opportunities for our imagination set before us by the Church! The illustrated manuscripts, altarpieces, and paintings for churches of the Ages of Faith remind us how much richer the celebration of the season was to our ancestors. For many today, once the body has been sated with food and drink, and the presents opened on Christmas Day, there is nothing more, nothing on which our soul can feed. For many without the Faith, the aftermath can be the most depressing time of the year. It can be almost worse if you sense a possibility which you feel unable to stretch out and grasp.

And what further opportunity is provided for us by the Church a little later in the season of Lent, when we may hope to make good progress in our Faith, by stepping up our spiritual training. We are offered these weeks to help us win a better mastery over our will, and hence be more responsive to God's grace and the needs of our neighbour.

If you can manage a retreat during Lent, this should be a big help in deepening your relationship with Our Lord, Our Lady and the saints, just as staying with friends for a few days can build up your friendship with them.

If your family and other commitments allow, it can also be splendidly enriching to spend a part of Holy Week before Easter in retreat. But in your early years as a Catholic you may feel it more appropriate to experience this sacred time in your parish. For this is when your parish priest takes his flock through the passion of Our Lord, reminds us again of what He suffered for us on Good Friday, helps us to see how God still suffers from our sins, and builds up the liturgical framework in which we will celebrate the joy of Easter.

Holy Week is also when you will begin to become familiar with the devotions of the Stations of the

Cross. To some converts, this may seem a rite which crushes the spirit. But it can help us understand the nature and meaning of physical suffering in the world. Only the Christian religion provides a satisfactory explanation of this. For it shows that we have a comrade, God himself, in the form of the second person of the Blessed Trinity, who has been before us in suffering, and His suffering, all undeserved, was of a most barbaric and humiliating kind. The Stations of the Cross can be a vivid and powerful reminder of this reality.

Moreover the Stations of the Cross can also help strengthen us for the kind of physical suffering which so many of us will have to face some time later in our lives. The ceremonies may also help us learn how to offer up to God our own sufferings, as a sign of love for Him and for others, so that none of our experiences can be considered wasted.

All Catholics then should set aside some time in Lent and Holy Week to attend the liturgy of the Stations of the Cross. But I suggest that you also allot a little time to make the Stations on your own. Almost all churches have a set of the fourteen stations on their walls. You might like to walk around them by yourself reflecting on Our Lord's journey to Calvary. There is something very intimate and personal about carrying out this devotion on your own. For those of you who would like to use a text on such a venture there are some brief sentences for each of the Stations in the Catholic Truth Society's *A Simple Prayer Book*. The Section is headed the Way of the Cross. There is also a more extensive version in Bishop Challoner's *Garden of the Soul*, where the text is based on prayers of St Alphonsus Ligouri.

In the Christian life, as in most aspects of human life, the full joy of any celebration is only achieved with adequate preparation. And the Church has sought to ensure that we are all properly prepared before the great feasts of Christmas and Easter arrive. As a newcomer to the Church you will want to take full advantage of these opportunities. In particular make sure that you attend the Easter Vigil, as well as the Holy Mass of Easter Day.

At the Vigil you will hear a deacon, if there is one in your parish, read or chant the wonderful paschal proclamation. This reminds us of all God, in His mercy, has done for the human race throughout history. We also have the opportunity at this time to renew our baptismal vows. This is especially important for those whose original vows were made by their godparents when they were babies. Our fervour should also be rekindled by the ceremonial lighting of the new fire, and the passing of the light on to others, by lighting each other's candles. This will help remind us of our duty to pass on the Faith.

Because Easter is such a special season of joy it is a particularly good time to celebrate with our friends. Christmas is a time when family links are naturally strengthened. This seems very fitting because the focus of this feast is very much on the Holy Family. Easter, by contrast, may provide an opportunity to stress friendship. It may be a good time to bring to your friends something of the joy you have in your Faith. It is worth taking some trouble to thinks of ways of sharing this celebration with them. At least once in your life you might consider going with a friend or group of friends to spend Holy Week and Easter in Rome. If your friends see something of your joy at Easter, they may be a little readier themselves for the gift of the Holy Spirit by the time Pentecost arrives! By which time also you yourself may be strengthened to help bring the Faith better to others.

Perhaps because it is no longer widely celebrated, or even noted by the average Briton, I have come to treasure the Feast of the Ascension. Since it always falls on a Thursday, those with paid jobs will usually be at work, unless they take time off. If you are at work, this is a good opportunity to take courage, and reveal to those with whom you work that you are Christian.

As it is a Holyday of Obligation, you will need to find an opportunity to hear Holy Mass, perhaps during your lunch break. A brief reference to your intention may be a way of revealing your Christian commitment, and could lay the ground for discussing the Faith at a later date. You may even find a fellow Catholic whom you can take with you on your visit to Our Lord. If you do a little research beforehand, and you are lucky, you may discover that there is a church which has one of the great musical works written especially for Ascensiontide in its liturgy for the day.

There is a good story about the value of acts of friendship of this kind. In the days of sail in the decade after the Napoleonic Wars there was a young merchant seaman called William Ullathorne. One day, while his ship was in a foreign port, the ship's mate suggested to the young Ullathorne that he accompany him to Holy Mass. Ullathorne agreed, and the experience brought him back to the Faith in which he had been brought up. He changed his life completely, began a period of study for the priesthood, was ordained, and was sent to serve as chaplain in New South Wales. Here his parishioners were mostly convicts who had been transported from Britain. Ullathorne made a major contribution towards the abolition of the evils of transportation; then, much later, he became a famous Archbishop of Birmingham.

You will be regularly thinking of Our Lady whenever you say the Rosary. But it is good to do something extra in the month of May which is dedicated to her. In the Northern hemisphere the new flowers remind us of Our Lady as the Mystical Rose. It was she who gave birth to Our Lord, who gave us our spiritual spring-time. A good pious custom is to recite the Angelus each day, and you might choose this month to begin this practice.

The angelus is a short prayer which is based on the greeting which the Archangel Gabriel gave to Our Lady when he told her of the coming incarnation of Our Lord. The Holy Father, and many clerical and lay Catholics, try to recite it at noon each day; some recite it also at 6 am in the morning, and at 6 pm in the evening. Certain churches and monasteries have the lovely custom of ringing a bell at these times, to remind the faithful of the incarnation. Few things turn our mind better to prayer than hearing the angelus bell being rung across distant fields. Those who work where there are no church bells may have to devise their own ways of reminding themselves of eternal things in the midst of their daily routine. People use all kinds of devices to do this. Setting an alarm on your watch may draw unwanted attention to yourself in an office or factory! Something crossed on you desk or workbench may help remind you unobtrusively of the time for a few minutes prayer.

The text of the angelus prayer is in an Appendix. I have given it in its English and Latin versions. For consistency I have used the thee and thou in the concluding prayers, since the Hail Mary uses this form. But often the angelus is recited with you and your, followed by the Hail Mary with its thou form. Friends who are together at the times for the angelus sometimes say the versicle and response in turn, so I have indicated these. Saying the angelus with a friend or friends can be like a foretaste of eternal life.

As I have already indicated, May can be a wonderful month to be received into the Church, because of its association with Our Lady. Although being received at Easter is much hallowed by tradition, there is something particularly apt about being received when Spring is at its peak. Much of your instruction may perhaps have taken place the previous autumn. You will have become acquainted with the liturgy in Advent and at Christmas. You may have been on a retreat in Lent and have deepened your Faith in Holy Week and at Easter. A little further preparation under the inspiration of the Holy Spirit, and you will be ready for your reception under the loving maternal care of Our Lady.

Getting to know Our Lady is such an important part of acquiring the full Catholic Faith, and such a powerful way of keeping it, that it really can be an excellent way of getting off to a good start to be received during a time when she is specially remembered. If, for example, you were received on the 29th of May, the Feast of the Visitation, which commemorates Our Lady's visit to her cousin, St Elizabeth, you would always have a reminder of your reception each time you say the Second Joyful Mystery of the Rosary.

A most attractive custom in May is to make a special pilgrimage, with members of your family or friends, to a shrine or church dedicated to Our Lady. Of course it is also one of the traditional months for a pilgrimage to her major shrines at Lourdes, Knock, Fatima, Walsingham or Guadaloupe. You may well want to go on one of these one day. But if you are not able to venture so far, a visit, perhaps with a picnic, to a suitable place dedicated to her, will provide a chance to show her special devotion and affection.

This pilgrimage can be an occasion when we remind ourself that it was this perfect human being, whose consent to the proposition of the Archangel Gabriel, set the whole process of our redemption under weigh. Those who have spent some time in parts of the world untouched by the Church, or where Catholic influence is weak, will, if they are at all reflective, be specially conscious of the need to remember the importance of the Incarnation, and all that flowed from that. A pilgrimage might be an opportunity to say the full fifteen decades of the Rosary. You might add to this the lovely litany of the Blessed Virgin.

All Catholics are regularly strengthened by attending Holy Mass, and frequent communion is now encouraged. It is therefore a great joy that the Church has provided us with a special opportunity in the summer to express our thanksgiving for the great love which Our Lord has shown us, by leaving with us His presence in the Blessed Sacrament. We cannot remind ourselves too often that we have Him still with us, in His Sacred Body and Blood, under the appearance of bread and wine. The great feast of Corpus Christi, a Holyday of Obligation, which the Church celebrates in May or June on the first Thursday after Trinity Sunday, is our chance to give special thanks for this supreme miracle. If you are lucky, your parish may have a procession to honour Our Lord in the Blessed Sacrament.

The summer months of June and July are rich in opportunities for celebrating the saints. For the English, there is the feast of their two great martyrs for the Faith, St Thomas More and St John Fisher on the 22nd of June. Near their feast is a good time to visit one of the great centres which kept the Old Religion in the time of Catholic persecution. Some of these have been depicted at the beginning of each chapter.

On the 24th of June there is the feast of St John the Baptist's birth. It was he who prepared the way for Our Lord, and had the strength of character not to be envious when the crowds turned their attention to Him.

For those who have had difficulties in accepting the grace of Faith, there is also the chance to honour St Thomas on the 3rd of July. This was the saint who doubted Our Lord's resurrection until he saw the Five

Wounds, and realised that He was both his Lord and his God.

A visit to a monastery or convent on the 11th July, or thereabouts, could be an excellent way of thanking God for St Benedict, the great saint of Western monasticism. It was his profound influence which spread the Faith, and shaped the development of mediæval Europe.

The two great women saints, St Mary Magdalene and St Martha, who knew Our Lord, and played such an important part in his earthly life, are commemorated on the 22nd and the 29th of July. Many women will be particularly encouraged by their example, and wish to show them special devotion. It is worth recalling that, apart from St John, it was the *women* in Our Lord's life who stood by Him to the end at the foot of the cross, and it was St Mary Magdalene who was given the privilege of being the first witness to His resurrection.

Those whose imagination is fired by the work and example of the Jesuits might visit a church in their charge on the feast of St Ignatius Loyola on the 31st of July.

One of the greatest feast of the summer, and a Holyday of Obligation, is the Feast of St Peter and St Paul on the 29th of June. St Peter was our first Bishop, and he and St Paul were martyred in Rome, so a visit there would be a splendid way of celebrating their glory. To be present at High Mass in Rome on their feast was the object of Hilaire Belloc's pilgrimage, which he describes so enchantingly in *The Path to Rome*. When a visit to Rome is not possible, a good way of marking the occasion could be to visit the cathedral of your diocese. In this way you would be emphasizing your personal allegiance to your bishop, and reminding yourself of his links to the Holy Father, the direct successor of St Peter.

Although the reason for honouring both St Peter and St Paul on the same day is hallowed by tradition, the great importance of each of them, makes it hard for the ordinary Christian to find a way of celebrating both worthily at the same time. It is well worthwhile, therefore, spending some time before the feast in preparing for it, and devising your own way of adequately honouring both great saints. One way of doing this might be to make a special effort to study some of their epistles. So much of our tradition and understanding of our Faith comes from these. As we read what they wrote, we might remind ourselves how close they were to Our Lord, and what a marvellous act of Providence it was that we have been left their writings as a means of building up our Faith.

This is perhaps an appropriate point to say something about the reading of Sacred Scripture. Nowadays Catholics are given plenty of encouragement to do this. There was a time when this was less so. Some Protestants have taken this as a reluctance by the Church to allow the faithful to examine scripture objectively for themselves. It is important that converts understand something of what lay behind the Church's past attitude. As you will have learned, the Catholic Church regards the Old and New Testaments as written under the guidance of the Holy Spirit. As you read Sacred Scripture, you should always try to have this aspect in mind. When you take up these books you should therefore always seek to put yourself in the presence of God.

Treating Sacred Scripture just like any other book can easily create a frame of mind that might, over time, weaken the Faith. This fear that ordinary people might lose their sense of awe in the presence of Sacred Scripture, was undoubtedly a factor which made the Church reluctant to encourage its reading in such a way that it became commonplace. In the past, particularly at the time of the Reformation, there was also a fear, largely justified as it turned out, that individual study of scripture could easily lead those not fully trained in the tradition of the Church or its theology, into error and religious exaggeration.

It is important, therefore, when reading Sacred Scripture, to read it, conscious that it is inspired by the Holy Spirit. We should also read it with the aid of a good, orthodox commentary. For the four gospels, the Acts of the Apostles, and some of St Paul's letters, particularly good commentaries are to be found in the paperback editions of the Navarre Bible. The text of the Bible used in these is that of the Catholic edition of the Revised Standard Version; the English text is set alongside the Latin of the New Vulgate of Pope John Paul IInd, a revision of the venerable Latin Vulgate of St Jerome. In this way you have a reference point for the language known to our Catholic forbears.

I would urge you to read some Sacred Scripture each day. There are two main ways of tackling this. One way would be to plan a scheme with your spiritual director. If you prefer a ready-made programme, I suggest that you follow the readings for Holy Mass each day in a missal. This will help you keep abreast of the liturgical events of the day, even if you are not able to hear Holy Mass. But you might also like to undertake a programme of what is called *lectio continua*. This is a programme of serial reading which takes you through the books of the Old Testament and New Testament over a period of a year, in the case of the New Testament, or several years, in the case of the Old Testament. There used to be a lectionary which covered both the readings for Holy Mass and *lectio continua* published by the Catholic Truth Society, but this has been discontinued. Unless your spiritual director can help, or you feel able to devise your own scheme, there is currently no alternative to looking out for a suitable non-Catholic scheme.

In addition to the daily reading of Sacred Scripture, you should enhance your piety by example, by reading about the lives of the saints who are commemorated on almost every day of the year. To do this properly you will need a book of the saints, with a calendar which tells you which saints are being remembered on which day. There are a large number of possibilities: two satisfactory ones, which are easy to come by, are: *A Dictionary of Saints* by Donald Attwater, and *Today We Celebrate* by Dom Gerard MacGinty OSB.

These two books are rather different in approach. Attwater gives concise lives of a large number of saints: Orthodox, Armenian, Anglo-Saxon, Celtic, as well as those well-known in Western Christendom. You will sometimes have six or seven brief biographies of saints' lives each day, although for many there are only a few brief lines. Dom MacGinty's book picks out the major saint for the day. He also provides us with a brief biography. But in addition he gives a short passage to read. This is sometimes an extract from the writing of the saint concerned, or a part of a homily or piece of devotional writing by another saintly or learned person, which is relevant to the particular commemoration.

In addition to Sacred Scripture and the lives of the Saints, you will want to extend your understanding of the Faith through additional reading. Your spiritual director will be ready to help with suggestions, and you may well develop ideas of your own. Your reading should have a dual purpose: to increase your understanding of the Faith, and to enable you to explain it better to others, so that you can act as a channel of grace to bring them closer to God.

All Catholics should make it a point of pride to read and study Papal Encyclicals as they come out. Although they are usually known by their Latin titles, they are always available in English. Not everyone will always be able to follow every aspect of them in their entirety. Those of the present Holy Father are rich in argument, and are often expressed in wonderfully poetical language. But they are not always simple, and some persistence may be needed. But the effort made will be richly rewarded. Once you get to know your parish priest, it is worth encouraging him to base a homily at Holy Mass on the main points of new encyclicals as they come out.

In addition to keeping up with the latest encyclicals, you should take the trouble to become acquainted with some of the most important earlier ones, especially those of the last one hundred years or so. Key encyclicals include the one by Pope Leo XIIIth on the Social and Economic Order, *Rerum Novarum* of 1891, which covers issues relating to the world of work. Another is *Pascendi Dominici Gregis* of 1907 in which Pope Pius Xth defends the Faith which has come down to us from the Apostles against some of the modern heresies which were beginning to afflict the Church at that time. Many of these heresies are still around. Pius XIIth produced two important encyclicals: the first on the nature of the Church, *Mystici Corporis Christi*, issued in 1943 at the height of the Second World War; and the second on false doctrines, *Humani Generis* of 1950, which reaffirms the Church's traditional theology and view of Sacred Scripture.

As I have indicated previously, all Catholics should make a special point of becoming acquainted with Pope Paul VIth's encyclical on Human Life and Sexuality, *Humanæ Vitæ* of 1968. The encyclical implicitly opposes the almost sacrilegious assumption that the majority of those who have received the grace of baptism and confirmation, and are regularly strengthened by the Sacraments of Our Blessed Lord, are incapable of exercising their will, so that they act in fulfilment of the commandments of God. Modern men and women are thus being treated by opponents of the encyclical as feeble creatures, who are almost of a different species from so many of their predecessors in the Faith, who have valiantly followed the Church's teaching throughout history.

Many of you will also want to read the most beautiful encyclical of the present Holy Father on the role of Our Lady, *Redemptoris Mater* of 1987. In this Pope John Paul IInd gives us some of the thinking behind his great personal devotion to her, and encourages us to share this.

But it is really invidious to single out only some encyclicals for special mention. Everyone will have their own favourites, which speak to them personally. It is amazing how, though written at different moments in time, and of widely different styles, they complement each other so well, and continue to be as relevant for us today as for the specific times for which they were written.

But in addition to Sacred Scripture, the lives of the saints and the papal encyclicals, you will want to extend your reading into other spiritual literature. I would urge you to delve into some of the great classics of the past, before you turn to the mass of modern books which weigh down the shelves of the modern Catholic bookshop. In your early reading, you might seek some acquaintance with the work of St Augustine, the Rule of St Benedict, the writings of St Bernard, St Francis of Assisi, and of St Francis de Sales.

Try reading too the work of both the great St Theresas: St Theresa of Avila, the towering Spanish mystic who was also an immensely practical religious reformer; and St Therese of Lisieux, the young nun who showed the way in which the little actions of a most ordinary life could lead to sanctity. I would also suggest you get to know the writings of St John Vianney, the saintly Curé d'Ars, who had such a keen understanding of human souls.

When you are ready to turn to more modern writing a good starting point is that of Cardinal Newman: his Meditations and Devotions are an excellent place to begin; I have also learned a great deal from the work of Monsignor Ronald Knox.

Not all of the works you will want are readily available in modern Catholic bookshops. The Catholic Central Library in London is not expensive to join, and is useful for those living or working in or near London. For purchases of older works not in paperback, John Bevan at Great Doward, near Ross-on-Wye, will probably be able to find you second-hand copies, if given a little time.

A particular favourite writer of mine on religious topics, whose work is alas, hard to come by, is the Victorian, Kenelm Digby. He was a convert to Catholicism in the 1820s, long before the Oxford movement brought a flood of young Anglicans into the Catholic Church. He was a physical giant of a man, who effectively founded the modern sport of rowing when he was an undergraduate at Cambridge just after the battle of Waterloo. He had learned his river boating from ferrymen when he lived by the Thames during his boyhood.

After graduation Digby subsequently wandered all over Europe like a gipsy, mostly on foot, sleeping rough in the open, or in barns, or in the poorest inns. During his journeys he reflected on the loss of Christian values which had occurred in the wake of the worship of "reason" in the 18th century. France was still coming to terms with the consequences of its revolution, and the terror in which so many, including priests and religious, were guillotined, and with the end of the domination of Napoleon.

It was the monasteries and churches of Europe which captured Digby's imagination. This hint of a nobler past led him to begin to read the writings of the great days of mediæval Christendom. Many of these works, which were in Latin or early European vernacular languages, lay hidden away in monastery libraries, still in their original manuscripts.

What Digby began to see in these writings was not just fine tales of the romantic past, but men and women engaged in the struggle to live the Christian virtues, as reflected in Our Lord's Sermon on the Mount. Of course, Digby recognised that the material lot of many mediæval men and women was hard. But the thing which fascinated him, and came to obsess him, was how many of them kept struggling to lead a good and holy life in accordance with the teachings of Our Lord. Some behaved very badly too, and were violent, cruel and uncharitable. But their writings showed him that many of those who were like this *did* repent of their sins, and *did* seek to amend their lives and return to the Christian virtues.

Digby found this an enormous contrast with the general tone of his own age. For in the early decades of the 19th century when he was young, most men and women, in all ranks of society. had stopped even trying to pursue anything remotely resembling Christian virtues; they were devoting their lives to self-interest, and the pursuit of sensual and material pleasures, as are so many today.

As a result of his travels and reflections, Digby wrote his first major work, *The Broadstone of Honour*, a four volume study of the values of mediæval Christendom. He followed this up with the massive eleven volumes of *Mores Catholici*. This second work illustrates, from original sources, the way in which mediæval men and women sought to live the Beatitudes. Digby was extremely learned and skilled in languages. Perhaps naively he assumed that all his likely readers would be similarly able to cope with large untranslated extracts from original sources in Latin, classical Greek, French, German, Italian and Spanish.

Digby was well-off, and his writings were printed privately, so there was no requirement for his works to attract a wide readership. But they became known to many of the key opinion formers in Victorian society. *Mores Catholici* was followed by *Compitum*, a further look at the institutions and customs of the Ages of Faith, as he called mediæval times. The seven volumes of this work show how Catholic Christianity enriched all these aspects of mediæval life.

Digby's great contribution was to let mediæval writers speak for themselves. He quoted extensively from original sources, rather than summarising or paraphrasing. The devotion, which is revealed in the mediæval writings Digby assembled, shines as brightly as the colours in those stained glass windows, which mediæval glaziers were putting into the churches and cathedrals at the same time.

A few may even be lucky enough to find a copy of Digby's *The Chapel of St John*, which contains a portrait of his beloved wife, Jane Mary Dillon. This seems to me the finest picture of Christian love between a husband and a wife in English literature. To read of such love, so finely expressed, can be a powerful inspiration to pursue such an ideal in your own marriage. It can also encourage you to seek the grace to sustain this ideal, just as the reading of the imperfections of married life, which bulk so large in modern fiction, can weaken your readiness to struggle to perfect your marriage.

Of course those who lead busy lives, or have demanding jobs, will be obliged to limit the amount of spiritual reading they do. In my experience a little, regularly each day, is better than great binges of spiritual reading, followed by weeks without anything at all.

It seemed appropriate to deal at some length with

spiritual reading when we were considering the celebration of the Feast of St Pater and St Paul in the liturgical year. The climax of the summer comes with the Feast of one who left no writings of her own, but was yet the most perfect of human beings.

The feast of the Assumption of Our Lady is on the 15th of August. At this feast we celebrate the triumph of that perfect human being, who was chosen by God to be His mother when He came among us as a human being. I rather regret that the celebration of this feast in England does not always quite have the grandeur and fervour which it has in many countries, which have always been predominantly Catholic. I pray that we will see further efforts made by the Church in Britain to enhance its celebration.

At the end of September, there is the feast of the three archangels, Michæl, Gabriel and Raphæl, who played such a prominent part in the history of salvation. All Catholics should be encouraged by the existence of these spiritual beings.

The month of October begins with Rosary Sunday. This was first celebrated following the Battle of Lepanto in 1571. In this battle the forces of the Christian West under Don John of Austria, aided by the prayer of the rosary of the ordinary soldiers and sailors, won a great naval defeat over the Moslem Turks, and hence preserved Europe for Christendom. Without this help, it is very likely that our civilisation would now be Islamic. The month continues with special devotion to Our Lady, which, in many parishes, takes the form of public recitation of the rosary.

November begins with the feast of All Saints on the Ist, again a Holyday of Obligation. Many saints have a particular day of the year in which they are specially remembered. The feast of All Saints gives us another opportunity to remember all those to whom we have a particular devotion; and not only those for whom the Church has set aside a special day, but others whose feasts are not marked in the universal calendar. On this occasion we have the chance to remember all the company of heaven, many of whom are known only to God. For the canonised saints are likely to be only a tiny proportion of that great crowd of witnesses, which no man can number, who are united with God in heaven.

The day following All Saints' Day is All Souls' Day. Every year on this day we should make a special effort to pray for the souls of our relations and friends. We do not know for certain what their destination has been after death. But it is a pious practice, sanctioned by tradition, and encouraged by the Church, to pray that, if our loved ones are in purgatory, they may be united with God as soon as it is fitting; and if they are in heaven, that they may do what they can to help keep us on the right path to the eternal home which God wishes for us all.

As autumn becomes winter, we are nearing Advent again. We ought now to be planning a retreat for ourselves, perhaps in the company of some member of our family or a friend. The practice of going on retreat is well-established among Catholics and is now also common among Christians of other traditions. Some other religions also encourage their members to spend a little time apart in prayer, and in more intensive spiritual exercise. As a new Catholic, you will want to consider with your spiritual director the possibility of a retreat, how long this might be, and where you might go. Catholics are not required to make an annual retreat. But many of them do so, and derive great benefit from it.

Traditionally Advent and Lent are favoured times for retreats, although you can, of course, go on retreat at any time during the year. Religious congregations of monks and nuns often receive lay people for retreats.

Some dioceses also have their own retreat houses, and sometimes parish priests will organise a retreat for members of their flock.

Retreats can last a day or two, or much longer. They may be highly organised, with a large number of talks or suggested themes for meditation provided by a retreat leader, or the staff of the organisation in charge of the retreat. Retreats with religious congregations, such as the Benedictines or Cistercians, who say or sing the Divine Office, usually make it possible for those on retreat to take part in this liturgy. It is a wonderful privilege to be able to take part in their daily sequence of prayer.

If you can rouse yourself in the midst of the night in a monastery or convent, you may be allowed to take part in the particularly beautiful office of lauds, when much of the world is asleep; then if you can manage it you can rise again at dawn to hear prime before Holy Mass. Then there are the other wonderfully poetic offices, so particular to monastic life: terce, sext, and nones. A retreat in a monastery or convent will help you better understand and love the psalms, which are the basis of their public praise and prayer. At the end of the day you may attend vespers and compline before the Great Silence which envelopes the monastic life till the bell tolls for lauds.

Other retreats, which are not monastic, may well have a liturgical structure, but without these additional services. But you may have opportunity for corporate recitation of the rosary, making the Stations of the Cross, and taking part in benediction.

Some retreats are less formal in structure. The person on retreat may be left to organise his or her own spiritual approach in extended silence. For some, this can be ideal; others can find it difficult to make good use of their time without careful prior preparation.

A great attraction of a retreat is that there are long

periods of silence. Very often there is no conversation during meals, although sometimes someone will read aloud from a book on a spiritual subject. A short period of recreational conversation may be part of the rules, but, apart from this, silence, broken only by the words and music of the liturgy, and perhaps talks or homilies on the things of God.

Before a retreat it is well worth thinking of the major aspects of your life you will want to bring before God in personal prayer. But you will want also to be open to the Holy Spirit during the retreat.

Traditionally a retreat offers a time to reflect on

> your vocation as a Christian;
>
> the four last things - death, judgement, hell and the resurrection;
>
> the life of Our Lord.

You will want to consider all of these. But it is also an opportunity to make a planned approach to your spiritual reading. A discussion with your spiritual director may be helpful. Many institutions offering retreats have a good library. But it may be as well to take with you any key books you wish to study, in case these are not available. But beware of using the retreat simply as an occasion for indiscriminate reading of whatever takes your fancy, or catches your eye on the bookshelf.

Make sure that you begin your retreat with a good confession. Check whether there will be a priest available to hear confessions during the retreat. If not, be sure you go before you set out. If you can obtain confession on the retreat, try to receive this Sacrament early on. This should help you get into a good position to make the most of your time.

Retreats should have some spiritual aims. Of course merely experiencing a prayerful atmosphere, and having an opportunity for quiet reflection and meditation, is restorative. But I would encourage you to come away from a retreat with some good resolutions in regard to your devotional life, your relations with Our Lord, Our Lady, and the saints, your progress in the virtues, and your plans to bring the Faith to others.

A retreat is also a good time to consider whether you have a vocation for some particular work of Our Lord, over and above the sanctification of your ordinary life, which we should all be pursuing every day. The resolutions can be of wide variety: to communicate more regularly with distant family and friends, to offer spiritual advice and comfort to a friend on a regular basis, to say the angelus each day, to make a better examination of conscience regularly, to try to introduce the Faith to some agnostic friend. The resolutions should be precise, and within the range of your achievement at the time, and hence practicable. You will want to pray hard for the grace to put them into effect when you return home at the end of the retreat.

A good retreat before Christmas or Easter is a marvellous preparation for these great feasts. I am sure that you will find they will help make you better able to spread real Christian joy to others, and withstand many of the worldly aspects which overlay the feasts nowadays.

Before you attend a retreat, your spiritual director may well have advised you on the sort of retreat which would suit you best. There are a great many types: they can last a day, a weekend, a week, or even longer. As a new convert you might go on a shortish retreat to begin with. This may help accustom you to the general atmosphere, and get you into training for longer periods of silence. As with long distance running, it can help to begin with shortish goals, rather than try a full marathon when you first take up jogging!

Taking your Place in the Parish

I have now said a little about how you might approach your new life as a Catholic as an individual. But the practice of your Faith is something which you will be sharing with other Christians. They also, please God, will be making a similar struggle towards personal holiness. Much of this joint effort together will be centred on the parish.

Once you have become a Catholic you will find yourself with a whole range of new acquaintances. In due course some will become personal friends. But there are some obstacles to becoming acquainted with other parishioners. Many Catholic parishes, like the churches of other denominations, offer quite a wide range of times for services. This flexibility helps ensure that most parishioners have times for Church services which suit their different circumstances and commitments.

Although this flexibility is valuable, it can mean that those who attend one service regularly do not necessarily get to know others who attend other services. And if you and others use this flexibility and attend services at different times from week to week, you may find it difficult to get to know many other parishioners very quickly. Of course, if you have been through the catechumenate in the parish, you are likely to have established a nucleus of contacts by the time you are received.

In recent years the parish priest usually greets members of the congregation after Holy Mass and other services. Some priests will use this opportunity to introduce newcomers to others in the congregation. In some parishes lay people are given the job of welcoming those new to the parish. But some older priests still regard it as more important to occupy themselves with the things of God after the service, and save their socialising for parish visits.

Do not expect too much from your new Catholic acquaintances immediately. Some may need a little time to work out how best to welcome a convert into their midst. Allow grace to take its course. Sometimes it may be easier to strike up a conversation with members of your congregation in shops or the street of your village or town, once their faces become familiar, rather than after a church service. Gradually you will begin to recognise new faces. You may be surprised to discover that some people you previously knew quite well by sight are actually members of the same parish. Perhaps in time you may discover that some of them are converts like yourself!

If your parish priest, or one of his assistant priests, did not prepare you for your reception, you will want to begin to get to know him and his colleagues. Remember that priests are dedicated to Our Lord, and act in His person at Holy Mass, and in the Sacrament of penance. They should be given special respect for this reason. At the same time they are human beings, and have all our human frailties. You will want to get to know them (and some of their frailties!) as soon and as well as you can.

If there is more than one priest in the parish they will usually live together in the presbytery. You will want to know their address and telephone number, in case of emergencies. Some Catholics like to carry something written in their wallet or handbag, which indicates that they are Catholics. This note or card might also provide the name, address and telephone number of your parish priest. This is a useful precaution against an unforseen circumstance.

Some imagination is required when you begin to have regular contact with Catholic priests. Of course you will know the one who prepared you for reception quite well. But if your are anything like me, you will have been so preoccupied with the pressures of the conversion process that you will not have shown adequate understanding of him as a human being.

It is important to understand and respect how Catholic priests differ from other Christian ministers. The obvious difference is that they are not married. This commitment to celibacy, or the consecration of their life in this way, should affect how you think about them. Their whole life is specially devoted to God and those in their spiritual care. In the thrilling words of scripture they are priests forever after the order of Melchizedek. They do not have to divide their attention between their parishioners, and their wife and family. Of course most younger priests will still have parents, and nearly all priests will have relations for whom they may have some responsibility. But most Catholic families try to ensure that a priest in the family is relieved of primary family responsibilities, so that he may be mainly concerned with the souls of his flock. It is a wonderful thing to know that this is indeed the case, when you join a parish.

But priests need human affection, and all parishioners should go out of their way to offer them the kindness they show to close friends. They should be invited to meals, given small presents, and shown spontaneous acts of appreciation and affection.

Many outside the Church do not know that Catholic priests receive no salary at all. They receive their living expenses, and usually a car to help in their work, and some pocket money to buy clothes. But apart from that, nothing. A few priests may have some private income, or may inherit money from parents or relations. But you will frequently hear that many priests give a great deal of this away, or use it for their church, or to help pay for new ones. In my parish three new Catholic churches have been built in the last twenty-five years, with financial help from the clergy themselves.

You will know from your catechism that it is the duty of Catholics to support their pastors. It is important to understand fully that it is what you put in the collection each Sunday, or provide by way of covenant, which is the basis on which the priests in the parish live, and run their parish.

Many priests pride themselves on the simplicity of their lives. But it should be a matter of honour to their parishioners that priests never want for essentials to help them carry out their work effectively. This should mean that parishioners ought to know whether or not their priests have proper modern office equipment for the complex administrative work, which many are now required to do in running a parish. If this is inadequate, you should consider helping to do something about it.

In addition, more personal gifts of food or drink (if they are not teetotallers), or money for holidays, offered discreetly, can be a useful way of helping. The occasion for paying for special medical treatment for a priest is also something to look out for. You will find that many practices are already well-established in the parish for this purpose. But you should make it your duty to discover what they are, and play a good part in them, extending them if they seem inadequate, within the means at your disposal.

It should be a special point of pride of every Catholic to help ensure that their parish priest or priests receive a substantial sum at Christmas. This is the time when Catholic priests traditionally receive their personal offering. In making this annual gift, try to call to mind all the many spiritual benefits which the Church has given you during the year, as well as the cost of running the parish: church heating and repairs, the candles and sacred elements for Holy Mass.

You should also reflect on the expenses of running the presbytery and a car, as well as the administrative cost of keeping a significant organisation functioning properly. You should compare the amount you give with the amounts you spend on yourself, your family, on entertainment, and on maintaining, decorating and furnishing your own home. Such a comparison will help you make a realistic Christmas offering.

During the year you will also have the opportunity to make an annual contribution to Peter's Pence. This is the way in which you can make a personal contribution to help the Holy Father in his work for the Church. Peter's Pence has been collected by the universal church since mediæval times. When making your contribution, you should remind yourself that the Holy Father is the true successor of that Galilean fisherman, whom God himself, when here on earth in the person of Our Lord, established as the rock on which His church was to be built.

The tireless pastoral work of our present Holy Father, who has taken the message of Our Lord to almost every corner of the world, is one of the great blessings of our age. He has now launched a campaign to bring about the reconversion of Europe. Despite the commitment of many faithful, all European countries, which have traditionally thought of themselves as Christian, have been badly weakened by materialism and hedonism, and have lost that pervading spiritual fervour which was so powerful in the Ages of Faith. We should dig deep into our pocket or handbag to support the central administration of the Church, which assists the Holy Father's great work.

Your parish will also have regular collections for the charitable work of the Church, for missions, for running the diocese, and training priests. You should be generous in your support of these activities also. The future spiritual well-being of your fellow Christians and yourself depends much on the support which is received now, for developments which will bear fruit many years later. Depending on your age, that priest who will be responsible for you when you are old, or comfort you when you are dying, may not have yet even begun his training for the priesthood.

Your parish will also play its part in collecting money for national and international charities. When international disasters occur, a contribution to a fund organised by the Church can be a good way of ensuring that it gets where it is needed without delay.

But in addition to these acts of charity, which the Church itself specifically encourages us to perform, you ought to consider adopting some personal charities of your own, which have specifically Christian purposes. As you will by now know, alms deeds, as they are traditionally called, are one of the Church's three eminent good works, along with prayer and fasting.

Some care is needed in choosing a personal charity. It may be best to choose one which bears some relationship to the size of your contribution. If you are enormously rich, then a large national charity may be suitable. But if your contribution, of necessity, is modest or small, then it may be better to choose a charity in your immediate neighbourhood, or a small national one. You should certainly try to keep in personal touch with the objectives and progress of any charity you support. Your contribution, however small, should be regular, and paid on time. Remember that you can honour God by trying to do small things like this as efficiently as possible. Try to do a little more than just pay out money on time, by attending at least one of its functions or meetings a year, and reading any literature attentively. Your charities should also be regularly remembered in your prayers.

When choosing a charity, it may be as well to exercise the Christian virtue of prudence. This cardinal virtue sounds rather old-fashioned, and you may not hear too much about it in the homilies you hear in Church. Alas, many charities are poorly run and managed. I do not mean that they ought always to be run by professional administrators with a large staff, and the latest management techniques. Far from it. There are many small-scale charities which are very well run on a shoe string by a hard-working saintly individual, or team. They never spend a penny on themselves, but their accounting and managerial skills may be inspirational rather than of the text book variety. Many of these charities can be excellent to support.

But there are other charities, which are very bureaucratic and have poor cost control. A high proportion of the funds they receive is spent on their own administration and staff expenses. I would be particularly prudent before contributing to charities where the staff spend a lot of time in conferences or meetings, in co-ordination with other charitable bodies, or on training courses. Some charities can lose their way, and become bodies which largely provide for the self-development of their staff.

Unfortunately, church charities can also develop in this way. A visit to the office of the charity concerned, either its head office, or that of one of its regions, can sometimes help you identify whether a charity is of this type, or whether it is efficiently and modestly run. You will get a feeling for whether a large part of the contributions being made are being put towards the objectives for which it was created, or whether it is one in which money is squandered on unnecessary staff expenses, and the main aims of the charity are being swamped by other concerns. Tell-tale posters on notice boards suggesting political rather than charitable interests among the staff may properly encourage a potential donor to exercise some Christian prudence in his or her giving.

Early Days

As a new convert you will also want to be prudent in the way you conduct yourself in your early days in the parish. Avoid anything which might make a splash. Play yourself in gradually. Much can be learned by the patient observation of how others behave. Of course your models should be those who are devout, and show signs of practising the Christian virtues. You should draw particular inspiration from those men and women whose cheerful outward appearance shows that they realise that they are sons and daughters of God.

In due course a priest or lay person in the parish may ask you to do something in the parish. Do not be surprised if this doesn't happen for a little time. If you have had experience of arriving in a new church of another Christian denomination, you may remember being pounced on and dragooned into doing something for the church the moment you show your face at a service. You may therefore be a little disappointed at the initial reaction you receive from the clergy and your parish congregation. Some people will value this opportunity to settle in quietly; others may find it strange, even cold.

If this happens, the likelihood is that you are being left to find your own feet. But others will probably be quietly watching over you, perhaps even praying for you. If something goes wrong in your life, you may well be surprised how many friends you already have, who only seemed to be faces.

A few weeks after I was received as a Catholic I had to go into hospital for a bit of minor surgery. My parish priest, whom I hardly knew since I had not been instructed by him, visited me at a distant hospital as a matter of course. I am sure that if you have family difficulties, or the death of a member of the family or friend, the priest will expect to be contacted immediately, and will provide valuable spiritual and practical help.

A good way of getting closer to Our Lord, and to Our Lady and the saints, is to attend some of the extra services which are offered in the parish. This may speed up the process of becoming acquainted with other members of the parish. If you have a car, you might be able to offer to take someone without transport to one of these additional services. As I have already indicated, the parish may have special opportunities for saying the rosary together, as part of the special devotions to Our Lady in October; or there may be a service of Benediction to attend.

A convert should get to know Benediction. To know it is to love it. This is a service in which Our Lord, in the form of the Sacred Host, is taken from the tabernacle and displayed to the people in a precious vessel called a monstrance. During this exposition, as it is called, the congregation usually have an opportunity to sing St Thomas Aquinas' great hymn, "*Tantum ergo sacramentum*". This can be sung in Latin, or English, when the first words are "*Therefore we before Him bending, this great sacrament adore...*". At the climax of the ceremony the priest blesses the congregation with the Sacred Host. After this blessing, the congregation praises God in His Three Persons, and blesses Him for His Mother Mary, His earthly step-father, St Joseph, and for His angels and saints.

Benediction is another way of showing our love for Our Lord, and reflecting on the amazing loving-kindness of God. For not only has Our Lord redeemed us, and provided us with sanctifying grace at our baptism, and regularly again in the sacrament of penance; not only has He left us His Holy Spirit to guide His Church, and dwell in each one of us; but He has also given us His Son, for as long as our world continues, in the Blessed Eucharist. We can receive Him in Holy

Communion; we can adore Him in the Tabernacle whenever we enter a Catholic Church where the sanctuary light indicates that He is there; and we can also adore Him, with greater ceremony, at the service of Benediction.

Of course we can talk to Our Lord at any time, at home, in the office or factory, or out walking. And we should try to do so very often, practising what is called "presence of God" many times throughout the day, saying short prayers, and discussing our problems with Him. But Our Lord, in His love for us, clearly saw our need for something more physical, to aid our devotion. We still need Faith. He will not force us. To outward observance, the Sacred Body and Blood are still bread and wine. But once we have received the gift of Faith, what a treasure the Blessed Sacrament is! Whenever we pass a Catholic Church we can "make a visit" to Him! This proximity to Our Lord can be particularly consoling, and can aid our devotion.

Benediction then gives us this added joy of being able to feast our eyes on Our Lord, under the appearance of the Sacred Host. It is a superb way of strengthening our Faith, and banishing any lukewarm feelings. Moreover, the privileges of Benediction are open to all: children, those outside the Church, hardened sinners, those under instruction in the Faith, as well as those loyal subjects of Our Lord who wish to demonstrate their love for Him.

I hope that you will come to share my joy in Benediction. God who become man for our sake, can see the importance for us as humans, of that which can be seen and touched. Although I did not understand this at the time of my conversion, I now see that this emphasis on the material and visible is a powerful sign of the authenticity of the teaching of the Church. Benediction, like the lighting of votive candles when we make a special prayer for someone, is a visible image of something which is hidden, but nonetheless real.

Of course prayers outside church, or without candles, may well be just as pleasing to God. But there is something eminently human and childlike, and hence lovable and appealing, about combining our prayer with something tangible. He who gave us His Body and Blood at the Last Supper, and came to us as the Light of the World, understood perfectly the true need of humankind for such material reassurance.

Practising the Faith in the Family or Alone at Home

But taking your proper part in the parish is only one side of being a Catholic. It is important that your Faith is firmly established at home. This applies whether you live with others, or alone. Ronald Knox, in his fine book, *Retreat in Slow Motion*, stresses the need to "internalise" one's religion.

Your Faith is not something which you merely demonstrate to others by attending church. It is not like following a sporting team. It is something which is internal to you, something you think about when you are alone.

I often think that this is one of the major failures of much modern religious education of young people. Children are taken to church, schools have "religious assemblies" or "chapel"; young people are "married in church". But all too rarely has a successful effort been made to encourage children and young people to talk personally to Our Lord, Our Lady and the saints.

Somehow the God which comes across in much religious instruction is remote, or concerned with major issues like international poverty, or questions of global war and peace. He is not shown as someone concerned with such simple matters as how each one of us, every day, is making progress towards our eternal home, and helping our friends to travel the same path. This personal religion, which we practice on our own, is probably the most precious acquisition a young person can take from his or her education.

What we need to build up is a Faith which would be of value to us if we were compelled to spend forty years alone on a desert island, or in solitary confinement in prison. It is those small daily habits of personal piety which are at the centre of our Christian life: daily spiritual reading, if we have access to books; personal prayer; meditation of the life of Our Blessed Lord; the rosary; regular recollection of presence of God; examination of conscience; daily Mass if we can manage this; regular confession. Of course, all of this would not be possible if we were alone on a desert island. But we could build the basic structure, if we had made an effort beforehand, and had made good use of God's gift of our memory.

Within the family, or in groups of people living together, it is important to seek to establish some basic Christian practices. A first step might be to ensure that there is grace at meal times. This touch of formality at meals is desirable in itself; it can serve as a mark of respect for the person who prepared the meal. But more importantly it is a regular sign of gratitude to God for all his benefits. If you have prepared the meal yourself and are eating alone, it can add that touch of reverence which may encourage you to lay out the meal, eat it, and clear up afterwards with a little more care than you might otherwise be tempted to do.

Most families and groups of people adapt quite easily to grace at meals. Visitors accept it, and usually quite like seeing such a custom. With my family, and with Christian friends, I often try to keep up the practice even when dining out in a restaurant. You may find some waiters pleased that the business of eating is being taken seriously!

You should also consider having some reminders of

your Faith about the house. Every Catholic home should have a crucifix on display, and something which depicts Our Lady. You will also want to have some reminder of those saints for whom you feel specially devotion. A photograph of the present Holy Father is a useful way of reminding yourself of the need to remember him in your prayers. It may also encourage you to keep up with his teaching!

There is no reason why these mementoes should be confined to the inside of the house. If you have a garden, you might consider a plaque, or statue or piece of tiling with some sacred picture or symbol there. This might help those in the garden to have a double joy: that of the seeing the earthly beauty of God's creation, in the flowers and trees, and of having a sign of the heavenly beauty of the Creator of the Universe, or of those who have gone before us and done His will. Of course you will want to be sensitive to the feelings of others in the household, if they are not Catholics. But in most cases you are likely to find support and encouragement, if you approach the question tactfully, and with obvious sincerity.

For those of your family and friends who are not Catholic, a small gesture which might help them draw closer to God could be to mark the feast day of a saint, whose Christian name they share, by sending them a card. This can cause some simple pleasure, and give them an extra day to look forward to, as well as their birthday. In some Christian countries, it is the feast day of the saint whose name you share, rather than your own birthday, which is particularly celebrated.

Whenever a major feast of the Church occurs, try to mark these at home with some small sign of Christian significance. This is not difficult in families with some Christian background, however shadowy it may be, at the main feasts at Easter and Christmastide. But you may need greater imagination to find something appropriate for Pentecost, Ascensiontide, Corpus Christi, the feasts of St Peter and St Paul, the Assumption of Our Lady, Michælmas and All Saints' and All Souls' days. But the challenge can be good for our ingenuity.

Sending of cards is an easy way of reminding others of these occasions. You may well find it difficult to obtain something suitable for all the occasions you may wish to mark in some way. But persistence may sometimes be rewarded. Postcards from art galleries of pictures by painters of the events being celebrated can sometimes be appropriate.

I am sure that Catholics should ensure that *all* the Christmas cards they send, whether to Christians or not, should be unambiguously Christian. The secularisation of Christmas cards should not be encouraged by Christians. To fail to send proper Christian cards for this feast to those without religion is an opportunity missed for providing a tiny channel of grace.

Naturally, developing good pious practices at home can be much easier if there are a number of Catholics in the family. You might even be able to introduce the custom of saying the rosary together. Modern life sometimes makes any routines for the family as a whole difficult to establish. But if one or two members of the family could meet regularly for a quarter of an hour say once or twice a week, and say five decades of the rosary, experience shows that this can bring enormous blessings, both of a general kind, and as a means of preserving family unity. The practice might be easier to establish in a young family with small children. But husbands and wives alone together, and even groups of friends might consider trying it.

Some of you may be inspired to go further, and have your own oratory or private chapel. I have already mentioned that Monsignor Gilbey has demonstrated that an old boot room can make an excellent small chapel! Even a corner of a room might be simply furnished as an oratory. Family prayers were held in many households across the Christian denominations for long periods of our history. I have no doubt that they made an important contribution towards preserving the Faith, and helping everyone to practice the Christian virtues better than they otherwise might have done.

The creation of an oratory could give some scope for developing the æsthetic sense for the glory of God, rather than simply for your family's comfort, or impressing your friends. But the important thing is that this should be rooted in a strong commitment to the Faith, and a vow of lifetime devotion. Alas, we sometimes see unused chapels in some of our great country houses, where the pious practice of the ancestors has been abandoned by later generations. A neglected oratory or chapel, however charming it looks, is a scandal to the Faith.

I shall say something here about what you should do about attending the services of other Christian denominations, once you have become a Catholic. This can be a particularly difficult problem, where one person in a family has become a Catholic, and others have remained as practising Christians in other denominations. If you were previously a Christian of another denomination yourself, you will have to decide what to do about attending services of the denomination from which you came.

This matter needs handling with care and sensitivity. If some members of your family are practising Christians, but not Catholics, there will be times when you could accompany them to services in their church. Clearly weddings, baptisms and funerals are occasions when you would wish to do this. But there may be other Christian festivals where accompanying other Christians in the family may be appropriate. You should do this as an important part of family solidarity, but also in a spirit of ecumenism. Of course, you will need to keep up your obligations in regard to Holy Mass as well.

There is clear potential for grace within non-Catholic Christian denominations. Those who have been properly baptised as Christians have already taken the first step, even if they are hardly conscious of it, since it probably took place when they were babies. All Christians whose Faith is based on the Creed should be encouraged to persist in their faith and practice. Naturally you will always hope that, in God's good time, they will be called to go further, and be received as Catholics. Remember God's grace is all around them too, and your prayers can help!

In matters of religious difference, politeness, good temper, kindness, and manners, are essential. They are all part of the way we exercise the Christian virtue of charity. You will not, alas, always find these qualities exemplified by all your fellow Catholics, or by those of other Christian denominations. But keep your ideals high, and examine your conscience carefully, to see if you are living up to them. You should always remember the importance of not setting a bad example to non-Christians. Our pattern should be that of the early Christians. Of them it was said: "Look how they love each other".

Attending other Christian denomination services requires great tact and sensitivity. You should always pray for this before going to such a service, and during it too. At the same time you must take care that, in the interest of being thought tolerant, you do not suggest to others that you are indifferent in your allegiance. This would be to make light of the principles which you recognised when you were received as a Catholic.

For this reason you should never breach the

Church's ecclesiastical discipline. In particular, as a Catholic, you should not receive any form of communion from a minister of another denomination, even if pressed to do so in the interests of ecumenism and good fellowship. This would be sinful, and would be to dishonour all those who have struggled to keep the Faith as it has been handed down from the time of the apostles. Rather than doing this, I suggest that, while others are taking part in this part of the service, you remain kneeling in prayer, and continue to pray, as Our Lord did, that all Christians will one day be united in Faith.

The pain of not being able to receive communion together, particularly in a close family, can be considerable. A way of dealing with this is to offer up this pain to Our Lord, and ask Him to use it for the saving of souls, especially of those who live in communities which are divided in their Christian beliefs.

Practising the Faith away from Home

It is important that we make an effort to practice our Faith when we are away from home. I have already spoken of the value of pilgrimages and retreats. But for many people their ordinary work involves travel. As I explained at the beginning of this book, this has been the case for me. Most people these days also spend some holidays away from home, either in Britain or abroad. Your practice of the Faith must always travel with you.

Travel on business can often provide good opportunities to strengthen and refresh the practice of your Faith. It is sometimes easier to get to an early service of Holy Mass, or to vespers or benediction in the evening, when you are away on business, than it is at home. Family commitments may be less of a constraint. To walk to an early church service in a city which you do not know well, either at home or abroad, can often stir the imagination. Indeed, sometimes it is only in the early morning, or the evening, that you have time to relax, since many business schedules are often extremely crowded.

If you are in a country where a language other than English is spoken, try to acquire the text of Holy Mass in the local language. This will enable you to follow the service more closely. In this way you will also have the worldly advantage of becoming used to the sound and rhythms of the language, which you may have to use or understand during the rest of the day. In other words, devotion to Our Lord abroad can have some useful practical advantages too!

More advanced linguists may feel able to make their confession in a foreign language, although, in many big cities abroad, you will usually be able to find confession in English, if you are prepared to shop around, and plan this carefully.

Business travel mostly takes place during the week, so there are usually less opportunities to hear a full-scale choral Mass, which is usually reserved for a Sunday. But you might occasionally strike a Holyday of Obligation when abroad. This may be an opportunity to hear a foreign choir tackle something in the great Christian choral tradition. If it is an ordinary weekday, you should look out for an evening Mass or vespers.

Your hotel will often be only too glad to help you find out the times of services. Otherwise a little detective work on foot, or with a local newspaper, may be all that is necessary to obtain the essential details. If no service is possible, try to make a visit to the Blessed Sacrament. This is always a good way of beginning or ending the day. Alas, sometimes you will be frustrated. In some cities, churches do not seem to open early, and are locked again in the early evening.

A good exception is in Rome, where you can find Holy Mass well before first light in many churches, including in the catacombs beneath St Peter's. It is also the best time of day to see many of the buildings themselves, without a vast throng of tourists!

Much modern business travel involves a large amount of time in æroplanes or trains, waiting at airports or stations, or in travelling by car (or being held up in traffic jams!). It is sensible to carry a simple Catholic prayer book, a New Testament. and a rosary with you. This will help lift your heart from the often soulless surroundings, which can be a feature of modern travelling. Saying a part of the rosary can be a useful antidote to the boredom and frustration which travel delays can cause. It is also an attractive alternative to much of the rather unedifying printed and illustrated material on display at airports, railway stations and motorway service areas.

The little collection of books I have suggested you take with you will also be invaluable for those evenings alone in hotel bedrooms. The hotel will offer you a menu of entertainment on television and video, some of it less than ennobling. It may also provide opportunities to exercise or relax your body in a swimming pool, sauna, or health club. But you will be left on your own in regard to your soul, apart from some prompting from the Gideon Society bible. This is your chance to show that you are able to meet the challenge adequately, by drawing on your plan of life.

Holidays can provide a different challenge. Of course pilgrimages can be one of the best kind of holiday. But there may be good reasons why a pilgrimage may not always be an appropriate choice for a family, a husband and wife, or for a group of friends. You may decide that your children are at that particular stage of their development when they need some good exercise, or to see particular things to stimulate their mind or eye. You and your spouse may wish to spend a holiday in developing some particular joint interest. You may wish to work at something which may be of professional importance, such as improvement in a foreign language. Friends may have a special interest, which they want to develop together on holiday.

Nevertheless, you will want to think in advance how you can share your holiday with God. Consider carefully whether your plan of life needs modifying when you are away. Will there be a church near where you are staying? If not, you will want to ensure that you take with you appropriate books of devotion and aids to piety for use on week days. How will you fulfil your obligation to hear Holy Mass on Sunday or on a Holyday of Obligation? Might you not, while on holiday, make an even bigger effort to get closer to Our Lord? Don't forget your rosary!

A holiday can also be a challenging exercise in ingenuity in advancing the spiritual welfare of a family. You will need to think carefully how to do this, without stimulating resistance to God's grace. No mean challenge when you are dealing with young children!

The Charles Bridge,
Prague

CHAPTER FOUR

A NEW VISION

WHEN you first become a Catholic, I would urge you to deepen your knowledge of the great inheritance of the Church in the fine arts, in architecture, and in music and literature. Some of this will be familiar to many already, Christians and non-Christians alike. But your Faith will help you look on much of this with new eyes. Instead of simply acknowledging works in this tradition as appealing, you will begin to understand the feelings and thinking which inspired those men and women who gave these treasures to the world for the glory of God.

Becoming a Catholic can also enable you to rediscover artistic work which you may have previously only half-understood, and introduce you to what was previously outside your comprehension. Moreover, you will now see this as the faithful have seen it, from the time when it was first created, and not simply as a cultural enthusiast.

As you develop your love for the Church's liturgy, you will begin to understand better the great music written for it: Gregorian chant, Monteverdi's Masses and Vespers, the church music of William Byrd, of Vivaldi, of Haydn and Mozart, Schubert and Lizst, Rossini and Bruckner, Puccini and Elgar, Poulenc and Messiæn.

As I have mentioned, the Holy Father has allowed the old Tridentine Mass, for which much of this great music was written, to be celebrated again. I would suggest that all new Catholics take the opportunity to hear this form of the Holy Mass, and so become familiar with the text to which these great musicians were responding. Opportunities to hear this music within the context of the Old Mass are not always easy to find. But you may well like to seek them out.

Once you have heard liturgical music in its proper setting in a church service, I should be surprised if you did not increasingly find that, when you hear it later in the concert hall, or on disk or tape, no matter how fine the performance is, it has a whole dimension missing. What is lacking is the understanding and devotion of the congregation.

When you begin to see the fine arts through Catholic eyes, you are likely to want to know more about what lies behind the great religious paintings and sculptures of the past, what symbols represent the saints, or the different virtues, what points of history or doctrine are being expounded or explained in an altar piece, or in a stained glass window. You may also begin to enquire why a church has been built or decorated like it is.

The answers will give you a better understanding of the Faith, and a greater respect for the piety and devotion of those who have gone before you. And this will help you appreciate better the tradition which stretches back to Pentecost and the life of Our Lord on earth.

When you look at buildings, or the architectural features of a city, town or village, I would urge you to reflect upon their links with the Faith. In countries which have remained predominantly Catholic, there are still many visible links: the niches which sometimes contain statues of Our Lady or the saints, and which are set into the outside walls of private houses. Sometimes these are lit up at night with lamps or candles. The calvaries (representations of Our Lord on the Cross) at the edge of a village or town, or at a cross road, or on the wayside; the huge crosses on the top of hills.

Even in Britain, pre-reformation churches sometimes still have a few signs of the Faith of our forebears which were not despoiled. You may find a piscina, the little stone basin where the sacred vessels for the Sacred Body and Blood of Our Lord were washed. Or there may be a rood screen, from which the figures of Our Lord and Lady and St John, the beloved disciple, who was given charge of Our Lady after the death of Our Lord, have been removed. Sometime we also come across a place for a tabernacle, where Our Lord in the Blessed Sacrament was laid.

In some of our great houses you may also find an ancient chapel, or a part of the house where it was sited before it was converted to secular use. I have mentioned how thrilling it was to me to see one of the small number of houses where the Old Faith has been kept throughout the time of persecution. To a Catholic, a priest hole, where priests hid during the days when priests were in danger of their lives for saying Holy Mass, is not just an interesting historical relic. It is a reminder of what was required of those who went before us to keep the Faith. It should give us pause to think how we would have behaved in such circumstances. We should try to reflect on the extent to which we are currently living, with fervour and devotion, the Faith for which others died.

English pre-reformation literature is imbued with a

spirit of the Faith. There has been a certain tendency among some protestants to claim that some of these, such as Chaucer and John Langland, were in some way, pre-reformation protestants. But if you re-read them, you will, I believe, see that this view is misguided. G K Chesterton's splendid book, *Chaucer*, puts much of this into perspective.

While Shakespeare's personal religious convictions are complex and elusive, I am sure that you will also find new insight into his plays as a result of your new found Faith. It may help to remember that Shakespeare was writing his plays at a time of violent struggle between the protestant ministers, who were behind Queen Elizabeth I and King James I, and those English Catholics who were trying to keep England within the unity of Christendom. All this was at a time when Christendom itself was just beginning to recover from a titanic struggle with the forces of Islam in the East.

You may not believe that the tactics pursued by the Papacy in dealing with England during this period were wise. But seen through the eyes of Faith, you may perhaps begin to glimpse how tiresome the Popes and Catholic Kings of Europe must have regarded the persistence of religious separatism in England, in the face of what must have seemed to them the more important struggle for the survival of Christendom itself. Shakespeare's Othello sheds light on the background to this struggle, even though the emphasis is on the domestic tragedy. It is interesting to speculate on how a playwright in Venice, Vienna or Rome, which were closer to the combat zone, would have presented a story with a background of conflict between Christians and Turks in Cyprus.

Some of you may well want to seek out the less well-known writers who persisted in the Old Religion: in some cases this meant death, or exile. The poet, St Robert Southwell, who became a Jesuit and was hung, drawn and quartered for the Faith in 1591, wrote some lovely poems. They are all the more poignant now we know what his destiny was to be. Richard Crashaw, like few others writing in English, broke down our native reserve with his candid expression of his personal love of our Blessed Lord and His mother; his verse conveys a deep sympathy for the Faith in all its richness.

From his writings, Dryden's Faith seems more intellectual: a reminder that our Faith is consistent with our reason, as well as our emotions. Overall 18th century English literature seems little touched by the Faith. It can, therefore, be all the more exciting to discover little pockets of Catholic resistance to the so-called Age of Reason. We can catch glimpses of this in the private letters of those English families which kept the Faith. Many of these had to send their children abroad to be educated in Catholic countries, since English Catholic schools were outlawed. Young people were often separated from their parents for years at a time, and their only communication was by letter. The family loyalty and devotion these show are often very moving.

Some light on English Catholic recusants, as those who remained loyal Catholics are called, can be gleaned from the life and writing of their pastors in the 18th century. One of the most outstanding of these was Bishop Challoner. I have already drawn attention to his *Garden of the Soul*, a book of devotion which is just as valuable today as it was when it was first written. Those who need encouragement in the cardinal virtue of fortitude will learn much from this good bishop's life. Edwin Burton's two volume biography shows how Challoner's patient devotion to his flock, and carefully argued, but well- mannered writings in defence of the Faith, supported the tiny band of Catholics in England. Fines, restrictions on employment, the rationalism of the age, must have made the harvest very meagre indeed. He had many disappointments: the head of a great family, which had remained Catholic since the Reformation, perhaps tired of not being able to play any part in public life, conforms to the Anglican Established Church. Catholics in the surrounding district, who, for perhaps two hundred years, had attended Holy Mass secretly at the great house, now had nowhere to go.

Some, as a result, alas, abandoned the Faith. But others sought hard to find ways of keeping it. The rebellions in 1715 and 1745 to try to restore the House of Stuart, led to periods of increased Catholic persecution. But Bishop Challoner kept on patiently with his work. A few new converts helped to compensate for the sadness of the losses. In some ways Bishop Challoner must have resembled those bishops and priests in Eastern Europe in the long night of persecution and anti-religious propaganda.

The true harvest of those years came in the 19th century. George N Schuster's book, *The Catholic Spirit in Modern English Literature*, shows how this developed. The ground was prepared by Sir Walter Scott, who reawakened public interest in the colour and virtues of the mediæval past, even though he was not a Catholic. In his *History of the Reformation*, William Cobbett reassessed the effects of the destruction of the monasteries, and concluded that the English poor were in many ways materially better off, as a result of the monks' efforts, than they were, much later, when the agricultural and industrial revolutions got under weigh.

I have already mentioned the work of Kenelm Digby which Schuster singles out for special attention. Two of the major clerics of the period wrote on a wide range of literary subjects. Cardinal Wiseman, the first Archbishop of Westminster, wrote a novel, as well as works of oriental scholarship and literary criticism,

Cardinal Newman, in addition to his novel, *Loss and Gain*, about the story of a conversion, wrote *Callista: A Tale of the Third Century*, an historical novel on the early days of the Faith in North Africa.

You may also like to become familiar with the work of three nineteenth century poets who drew much of their inspiration from the Faith: Coventry Patmore, Aubrey de Vere and Gerard Manley Hopkins. This Catholic tradition in poetry was continued into this century by Francis Thompson. Thompson's life and writing have echoes of the life of that lovely canonised young Frenchman, Benedict Joseph Labré. Thompson wandered London dreaming and writing of the things of God; Labrè tramped all over Europe visiting the sacred shrines of Christendom, and by his example and holy death in Rome, drew many to the Faith, and a better life.

A more worldly writer, who was also a convert, was the American novelist, F Marion Crawford. He wrote novels in the last years of the nineteenth and the first decade of the twentieth century. He is an interesting cosmopolitan figure. His father was an American sculptor who lived and worked in Rome. The young Crawford was sent to Cambridge University, which he disliked, and then to Karlsruhe University in Germany, which he preferred. After University he became a journalist in India where he knew Kipling.

Crawford became a Catholic in the East, then returned to live with his widowed mother in Rome. In order to keep himself he began to write fiction. His novels were best-sellers and Crawford made a fortune which enabled him to live in great style in Sorrento in Italy. He was also a valuable source of revenue for the young Scottish publishing house, Macmillan & Co. Crawford's best books are either set in Rome in the last days of the Papal States, or are vivid and gripping historical tales of earlier Italian history. They provide a fascinating insight into the attitudes and values of Catholic Italy.

Crawford was writing at about the same time as Robert Hugh Benson. As I mentioned in Chapter One this fascinating figure was the son of an Anglican Archbishop of Canterbury. His two brothers were also well-known writers: the eldest was an essayist, literary scholar and diarist, who became President of Magdalene College, Cambridge. He is best known for writing the words of Land of Hope and Glory. His other brother, E F Benson, wrote novels of social satire which have recently been televised. Robert Hugh's work is more varied: he wrote plays, verse, sermons, and books of devotion. But every year, between 1900 and his death at the age of 43 in 1914, he also wrote one or perhaps two novels. Some of his historical novels have racy plots dealing with religious and political issues in Tudor and Stuart times. His fiction, set in modern times, treats some of the moral and religious dilemmas faced by Edwardian men and women. There are also two prophetic books about the future of England and Europe: *Lord of the World* and *The Dawn of All*, which are well worth seeking out.

No Catholic should need encouragement to get to know the writings of G K Chesterton. The range, wit, sheer good spirits, and profound moral seriousness of his novels, detective stories, biographies, poetry and newspaper articles, are reason enough to give much thanks to the Holy Spirit. There is good value too in the novels, books of criticism, verse and historical writing of his two friends, Hilaire Belloc and Maurice Baring.

Every Catholic should read Belloc's *The Path to Rome*. This is not the story of Belloc's conversion—he was born a Catholic—. It simply tells the romantic tale of how, one day, when he was before the statue of Our Lady in the parish church of his French family in

Northern France, he vowed to walk to Rome. He set out almost at once to fulfil this vow. His aim was to hear Mass on every day of his pilgrimage, and to be in Rome for the feast of St Peter and St Paul. Readers of *The Path to Rome* will have the privilege of being invited into the confidence of a great Christian soul and defender of the Faith. Anyone who can successfully address an election rally, as Belloc subsequently did as a Parliamentary candidate, while publicly brandishing a rosary, as a way of disarming anti-Catholic prejudice, must command our respect!

The fact that Evelyn Waugh is now generally considered as one of the finest writers in English since the Second World War, should encourage Catholics to become familiar with his work. He is perhaps best known for his humorous and sometimes rather cynical studies of the foibles of the middle and upper classes. But he has also written an excellent biography of the great Catholic priest, Ronald Knox. Greater riches are available from the work of Waugh for those who have some understanding of the Faith which was so much a part of his genius. *Brideshead Revisited* seems to me almost impossible to understand, except in the light of the Christian doctrine of grace. It is only by sharing this Faith that you can fully understand why Julia Mottram's self denial, in refusing to conform to the world's values by seeking a divorce, and marrying the hero, Charles Ryder, is bound up with her later charitable work; or why Sebastian Flyte's weakness of character could be redeemed into a kind of saintliness.

Those with a more philosophic turn of mind may well want to explore the main Catholic philosophical traditions, particularly the writing of St Thomas Aquinas, the 13th century Dominican. His system of philosophy had its origins in Aristotle, and is generally known as Thomism. It has had an enormous impact on the Western philosophical tradition, and is much treasured by Catholics. Indeed it is the only philosophical system which the Church has *recommended* as being in accordance with the Faith. This does not mean that all Catholic philosophers have to be Thomists. But it does mean that Catholic philosophers should understand St Thomas' main ideas.

Cardinal Newman's philosophy, which is in the tradition of British naturalism from Locke to Wittgenstein, is currently also having something of a revival. The widespread celebration of the centenary of Newman's death in 1990, and the Church's declaration that he is to be entitled venerable, a step towards his being declared a saint by the Church, has increased interest in all of his writings. Two books, *The Grammar of Assent* and *The Development of Christian Doctrine* contain some of the most important elements of his philosophical ideas.

Coughton Court

CHAPTER FIVE

HANDING ON THE TORCH

IF YOU have children, you will devoutly hope that your conversion begins a line of Catholics which will continue till the second coming of Our Lord. If you are not married, or are married without children, you will still wish to do what you can to act as a channel of grace to bring others in your family to the Faith. An isolated Catholic in a family is only a tiny harvest for Our Lord.

If you feel daunted at the prospect of trying to bring the Faith to others, it may be worth reminding yourself, if your family originated in a country with a Christian tradition, that at some point in the past one of your ancestors almost certainly joined the Church, then successfully passed on the Faith to his or her descendants and others in the family. If your family seems at first sight to be unpromising ground in which to sow the seed of Faith, you might think of the difficulties faced by others in the past: those seeking to bring a Roman or Greek pagan to the Faith, or a Platonic philosopher, or a Goth or Hun, a Nordic worshipper of Odin, a 18th century rationalist, a decadent of the 1890s. Remember that Our Lord, Our Lady, and the Saints are always at hand to help. All you are called to do is to act as the channel for the grace continually being offered by God to others in your family, and to draw on your own talents, to help rebuild this Catholic heritage.

Nor should you be disheartened by setbacks. The enemy has small tactical victories quite often. When a child of a long line of Catholics loses the Faith, or seriously fails to live up to its principles, this weakens the Body of Christ. It is worse when any scandal becomes widely known, as occurs when a prominent Catholic family is involved. This can provide the opportunity for those who oppose the Church to be scornful. The resolve of others who are beginning to respond to grace can be weakened. Those who wish the Faith ill, may well rejoice when a member of a well-known Catholic family gives up the Faith, and a long line of faithful followers of Our Lord is broken. Hardness of heart may give them pleasure to think of succeeding generations being brought up outside the Church. That is why causing scandal is so harmful. It may so easily cause others to stumble and drop the baton, which has been carried and passed on through so many generations. We need to help redress these losses, and we must never become disheartened. Our Lord's victory is assured. Always persevere.

Personal Example

What do you need to do to help bring others in your family to the Church, and ensure that their Faith is well-founded and permanent? The key to success within the family is personal example. Others need to see you as someone consistently making a sincere effort to live the Christian life, and following the teachings of Our

Lord. Your religion must not be something which you put on for others as a veneer, or just the pious practice of attending Holy Mass on Sunday, and on Holy Days of obligation, however essential that is. It must not just seem an æsthetic or social preference, or even just a matter of knowing about Catholic teaching. The Faith must be lived.

Unless the rest of the family comes to understand the way your Faith actually affects your behaviour, they may simply admire the self-discipline of your church-going, or your intellectual rigour. But they will not be attracted to the Faith as something vital which they need themselves.

They may even simply imitate your spirit of discipline in religion, in other aspects of their lives. They may go jogging regularly, or swim every morning for the sake of their health; or work persistently hard at their jobs to achieve worldly success, or become conscientious in the management of their personal affairs, in order to achieve self-satisfaction. But the main prize will elude them. For they have not come to see your Faith as the guiding principle which is at the centre of your soul.

For your family to share your Faith, they will need to identify it as the key to your thinking and behaviour. It is this which makes you seek to be less self-centred, more joyful, sounder in your judgement, and readier to pick yourself up after life's knocks.

This sounds as if you must put on a mask of perfection for the benefit of your family. On the contrary, they only need to see you as someone aware of his or her imperfections, but always struggling, and seeking God's grace to overcome them. They need to see how this struggle helps make you humble. They should see that you are aware, both of your imperfections, and of the greatness of God, and of the obligations which this knowledge imposes on you as one of His creatures.

In observing how you live your life, your family should come to learn the difference between this true humility, and a lack of self-confidence. For any self-confidence you have will be seen to arise, not from a trust in your own knowledge, skills and understanding, but from your trust in God; and your conviction that, with His help and the Sacraments of the Church, you are indeed able to do many useful things with your life, and to help the spreading of His kingdom.

To pass on the Faith within the family you will want to do everything in your power to avoid giving an impression of lukewarmness, or half-commitment. Your family will need to realise that you are always seeking to put others first, because you put God first. And you are putting Him first, because you know that it was He who put you first.

Your Faith, and your practice of the Christian life, will need to survive close scrutiny from those nearest you. They know all your weaknesses, as well as your strengths. One test of your sincerity, that your family is bound to apply to you, is the extent to which they are aware that you practice your Faith when you are on your own. The Faith is not something that you live just to encourage *them*, although you will fervently pray to be able to do this as well.

Practising the Virtues

In the earlier parts of this book I have suggested some ideas for your rule of life as a Catholic. Much of what I am now going to mention, you will have probably already learned in your preparation to enter the Church, or you will be told when you receive spiritual direction. But I believe that it is worth bringing together here, in the context of how you will need to be behaving, in order to pass on the Faith successfully.

In essence, to help you become an effective channel of grace for passing on the Faith, you will need to be practising the Christian virtues. As you will have learned from the Catechism, there are three theological virtues, Faith, Hope, and Charity, or Love as it is now often called. You will have been taught that they are in origin gifts from God. These are the supernatural virtues which are acquired by prayer and the sacraments. Without the gift of Faith you would not have been able to become a member of the Church at all. Without Hope, you may at times be in danger of being overwhelmed by despair, and losing the Faith which you have so carefully won. Without Charity, you will not be in possession of that which enables you to pursue the very end for which you have been created, which is to love God and our fellow creatures for His sake.

Once these virtues have been received, they need practising. This is both to help you live as a Christian, and to pass on Christianity successfully to others. The Sacraments, spiritual reading, and the other pious practices I have suggested, will play a useful part in helping these virtues grow in you.

But in addition to these theological virtues, you will also need to develop the four cardinal virtues. These are acquired by our own efforts and practice, although we may always pray to God for help in acquiring them. The cardinal virtues are the qualities which men need to live an effective life in human terms, whether or not they are Christians. But they are also needful for your practice of the theological virtues, particularly that of charity.

The first of these cardinal virtues is *prudence*. In effect this is sound judgement. It is the quality which enables us to make the important distinctions in life: discerning truth from falsehood, right from wrong, reason from emotion, fact from opinion. It also helps us decide when we need to make a stand, and when the issue is not a vital one of principle, but one on which several viewpoints are possible. It encourages us to weigh up the evidence, to take sound advice, then act. It is not prudent to be so cautious that we fail to act when we should.

Justice is giving others what is due to them. It is a reflection of God's justice. It is the quality by which we recognise the rights of others, including the rights of God. It is also particularly concerned with truthfulness and fidelity. In essence it is a true sense of responsibility.

Fortitude, or courage, is the quality which enables us to overcome or withstand hardship, inconvenience, disappointment, or pain. It has a physical, mental and spiritual aspect. It is a quality we may need if we have to face a long and painful illness, a serious disappointment in our career, the death of someone especially dear to us, or even a trial of our Faith. We need it to pursue the difficult good, to take that examination or test in which we are afraid we may fail.

Temperance is that quality of self-discipline or rational control of our passions, appetites and will, for the sake of some higher good. Without temperance, you will find the achievement of many of your higher goals will be impossible, whether they be worldly ambitions, or spiritual aims. Much of modern advertising, and what we see on television, hear on radio, or read in modern literature, encourages us towards self-indulgence, and the habitual pursuit of comfort and pleasure. To be able to meet most of our objectives, we need to acquire and continue to practice this virtue, so as to able to pursue our life's aims, whatever they may be.

Unless your children can be brought to develop within themselves a reasonable balance of these four virtues, it will be difficult for the Faith to be passed on to them successfully. Without *prudence*, they will not be in a position to discern between sound doctrine, and the flotsam and jetsam of other beliefs to which they, and their fellows, will be continually subjected. Without *justice*, they will not be able to see beyond themselves, to the rights and duties of their parents, of other people, of the community and the State, and to understand what is owed to God. Without *fortitude*, however sound their original judgement, and however well-developed their sense of justice and fairness, they will not have the persistence and toughness to keep going, when their worldly or spiritual journey becomes hard. Finally, if they lack *temperance*, they will tend to founder whenever they are confronted by sudden assaults of their emotions, and bodily appetites. Although they may understand, and even love the Faith, they may be easily tempted away from its ideals.

The cardinal virtues are not easily acquired. We will all find some of them easier than others. It is only by persistent encouragement and example that young people build up their characters on a sure foundation, which includes them all. Their acquisition is a lifelong process, and it is one which can never start too early.

The essential first step is to help your children begin to gain some mastery over their impulses and wills. A good way to start is to encourage them to practice waiting for things. Nearly everything worthwhile takes time, or needs waiting for. All of us have to wait for heaven. At first, you will actively help your children in the matter of learning to wait. But in due course they will need to learn how to impose this restraint on themselves.

Training the body and the will can be done for purely secular motives: to be better at sport, to perform better in your daily tasks, to get more out of your hobby. But how much nobler it is to make the effort for the sake of your immortal soul, and to enable you to play a more effective part in the redemption of the world.

The Christian technical term for bringing the body and will under control is the ascetical struggle. This is the process of learning to make acts of denial of the will and impulse, in order to be in a better position to rise to the really important challenges of life.

It is wonderful to discover that God's grace and the Sacraments actually help you in this. The regular habit of small acts of self-denial (not I hasten to add ones which are paraded before others), combined with the grace we receive in the Sacraments, are valuable preparation, both for helping us achieve our objectives, and enabling us to cope better with the difficulties in life we may have to overcome. In Her wisdom, the Church offers encouragement to help us with this, by giving us commandments in regard to fasting and abstinence. We should make proper use of these to help train ourselves in the virtues, and encourage our children to use these as opportunities for making moral progress.

It is unfortunately true that, once you have got into the habit of giving way to whim and impulse, it is hard to gain the mastery again. This is the reason why you need to encourage your children to begin training their wills early.

As they reach the age when they can understand reason, they need to be told about the reasons for self-discipline. When this is being done, they should be introduced to the idea that seeking control of their wills is a means of withstanding temptation to sin. It is a way of building up our loyalty to God and His Church, and of recompensing God for His love, and for our frequent neglect of His commandments, which He gave us for our good. Modern theories about the dangers of "repression" encourage us to give in to our whims and desires, rather than seek to control them. Those in other cultures, Muslims and Japanese, for example, know better, as did earlier generations of Christians.

We must come to see for ourselves that, unless our children learn to control their wills, they will find that their wishes and ambitions are frustrated by their own inability to pursue a steady course. This is one of the most important lessons of education, and it is one in which the basic grounding needs to be acquired within the family.

You love your children. But it is their eternal souls which matter most. Indulging your children, and weakening their wills may do them considerable harm. It may encourage them to be self-centred. Subsequently this tendency may contribute to a massive loss of self-confidence, when they realise that others in the world do not share their parents' view of their importance. Then they may discover, perhaps too late, that they have not the strength of character themselves to pursue their own objectives persistently.

The most important lesson a child can learn from you is to put God first. This puts all forms of self-centredness into perspective. As I have suggested, the best way of teaching your child about this is to set a good example yourself. After that, it is a matter of patiently helping them to acquire the virtues necessary to put their love of God, and of others for His sake, into practice.

The Faith and Children

You may be surprised that I have not so far mentioned the duty of a Catholic to ensure that his or her children are brought up in the Faith. The response to Question 201 of *A Catechism of Christian Doctrine* says: "The duty of parents towards their children is to provide for them, to instruct and correct them, and to give them a good Catholic education."

This requirement cannot be avoided or passed over

to another, while you are alive. What I have been attempting to do above is to set the framework to the first part of the response, that of instructing and correcting your children. This vital first stage, before the children go to school, is usually in the hands of parents, especially the mother.

This process of introducing the virtues should happen well before schooling. That is why you need to think carefully before trusting your child to a childminder, or a nursery school. You need to assess the values which are being introduced to them, particularly those which relate to learning to control their will. Parents need to be aware in detail about the moral assumptions behind what is being taught, when children are first put into the care of others, just as much as in primary schools, secondary schools, and at University. It is not just a question of the knowledge and skills which are being taught, but what training in character is being offered, or simply allowed to occur by default. Since the education of your children is your responsibility, you must know all about what is going on, and think carefully about it.

Carrying out the second aspect of the requirement in the Catechism, that of giving your children a good Catholic education, seems more straightforward. You might think that this will best be fulfilled by sending them to a Catholic school. There are independent Catholic schools, and voluntary Catholic schools, largely funded by the Government where there are no fees. As a parent, you will need to consider your responsibilities for the education of your children in the light of what you can afford (whether it is right for both parents to be away from the home earning their living, when the children are young, is one of the important issues).

But you also need to consider carefully the nature of the Catholic schools, which are possible on geographic grounds, or otherwise, for your children. The essential consideration is *not* the educational facilities at the school, its academic record, or even how well it teaches the doctrine of the Church, however important these are. It is how successful it is in helping its pupils live their Faith.

If your spouse is of another Christian tradition or a non-believer, you will also have to take this into account in determining a school for your children. You need to balance your duty to your Faith, and the sacred relationship of your marriage. If you are a recent convert, your spouse may well have made no commitment to bring up the children in the Catholic Faith. But you still have a requirement to give them a good Catholic education. How you work towards this must depend on the age of your children at the time of your conversion, and the wishes of your spouse in the matter.

You will need to pray for grace to help you resolve these issues in a way that neither harms the Catholic Faith, or puts your children's immortal souls at risk. A practical question may be whether you should withdraw your children from a non-Catholic school, and send them to a Catholic one. As well as the views of your spouse, you will need to take account of educational considerations, particularly in regard to timing.

There are other issues too. Should your children be baptised and if so, how quickly? This will not be necessary if they have received valid baptism within another Christian denomination. If they are not baptised you should make every effort to have this put right as soon as possible. Is it appropriate for them to be offered instruction? Again this is a matter you will want to discuss with your spouse and your parish priest. To prepare for this, you will need much thought and prayer. It is very important that there should not be a conflict between parents on this issue, as this will only confuse the children.

If you are not satisfied with the education being offered by local schools, Catholic or otherwise, you might even consider getting together with other parents to set up a new school. This is probably more common in some other countries than in Britain. A number of new ecumenical Christian schools have been set up in Australia, particularly in sparsely-populated country areas, where there are not many schools. Some of these have provision for orthodox Catholic instruction to the Catholic pupils. In Spain, Catholic families have also grouped themselves together to set up their own schools.

Outside your immediate family your conversion may well strengthen bonds with other Catholic relations, if there are any. Make sure you make something of this, but try to ensure that there is no development of "them and us" factions. Always remember the need to show the Faith in the best light as an ambassador of Our Lord. And remember that others will in future judge you partly as a Catholic, rather than just as an ordinary individual. Those who do not have goodwill towards the Faith may look out for reasons to find fault. For this reason, one of the most important things you need to show when dealing with your family and friends, is your joy in your new found belief.

Christian Marriage

The romantic ideal of valuing the beloved above all else in this life, even above God, is profoundly unchristian. A Christian should never put loved ones before Him, for it was *He* who gave *them* to be loved. Of course some may love their spouse above all other living creatures. To show your love for God, you love your spouse. The task for both of you is to get each other to heaven.

God takes people seriously. They are expected to

take their married vows seriously. Before a couple marry they need to be exercising all the virtues, especially prudence. The choice two people make needs to be fully considered, not simply a reaction to an infatuation. Christ restored the broken image of the covenant of marriage. The redemption has made Christian marriage possible. The covenant of marriage reflects that covenant between Christ and His Church. Christian marriage then is a vocation in Christ, like the priesthood, or the celibacy of a person who enters the religious life.

Your marriage should be creative and fruitful. Marriage usually gives a couple the chance to share in God's creativity through having children. Children are a kind of praise to God, and a prayer to Him. That is one reason why sexual relations should be potentially creative, and not artificially constrained by physical means.

If your marriage is not blessed with children, your vocation may well be elsewhere: to give a home to the children of others, or to give out your love to others. Perhaps your vocation is to look after the elderly, or those less fortunate than you in your community. You can still find ways for you to praise and pray to God as a couple united by love. With the help of God's grace, and strengthened regularly by the sacraments, married couples can all find the inspiration to pursue the high ideas of lifelong fidelity, purity and fruitfulness.

If, when you become a Catholic, you are already married, or you have been living with someone outside marriage, or are already divorced, you will need to discuss the matter with your parish priest. He will be in the best position to tell you what you should do in order to live as Christ wishes you to do.

With regard to passing on the Faith to your spouse, you must rely on prayer, your own joy in the Faith, and the grace of God. If your spouse remains outside the

Church, see this as an opportunity to bring the Faith to a wider circle, rather than as a handicap. It may be your chance to develop friendship with other Christians across the ecumenical divide, or to help those who are spiritually floundering. In your dealings with non-Catholic friends or your spouse, avoid controversy. State your position if this is required, but never allow an argument to develop. Marriage to someone who is not a Catholic may lead to conflicts over religious obligations: extra devotions, spiritual direction, or confession. The best policy is to be clear what your obligations are, explain clearly what you need to do, and stick to it.

But remember also that you also have family obligations. Just as you would not want to neglect your family for your work, make sure you don't neglect your family, which is one of your main Christian obligations, simply for the sake of religious solidarity. Pray about any situations in which you appear to be being pulled in two different directions. And remember always to discuss any seeming conflicts with Our Lord and Our Lady.

Being an Apostle

Once you begin to realise the full extent of the grace which Our Lord provides to members of His Church, you will want to pass on the Faith to others. Our Lord has asked us all to do this, as Holy Scripture makes clear. But some of us may be reluctant to take this request as seriously as we should. This may be partly because we feel inadequate for the task, and partly because we don't know how best to go about it.

Our feeling of inadequacy should not hold us back. We have received sanctifying grace at our confirmation; this is nothing less than was received by the first apostles. If our qualifications could be compared with theirs, a number of us would appear to be, in worldly terms at least, no less fitted for Our Lord's work than many of them.

Naturally we do need to consider carefully how we approach our task. We should seek the assistance of Our Lord, Our Lady, our guardian angel, and our favourite saints. An essential condition for bringing others to the Church, or apostolate as it is sometimes called, is our own struggle for personal holiness. Remember it is not necessary for us to *be* holy; only that we are continually struggling towards this goal, and picking ourselves up after any setback. It is only when we are doing this, and this is sensed by others, that our attempts to bring them to the Faith are likely to bear fruit. Moreover our work will be the more effective if we are able to show that our Faith brings to us the happiness of one who knows that he or she is a son or daughter of God.

The most effective way of bringing a lasting Faith to others is through personal friendship. We read in St John's gospel (Ch. 1.vv. 45 ff) that St Philip was so captivated by Our Lord, that he could not but tell his friend, Nathaniel. Rather than trying to answer detailed questions about Our Lord, St Philip simply invited his friend to come and see for himself. This should be our approach too. We should try to *show* our Faith to others in a direct, practical and human way, rather than by seeking to overwhelm them with facts or arguments. A brief visit with them to a Catholic church, where Our Lord is present in the tabernacle, may be a good supernatural way to sow a seed.

You will, at some stage, need to put your beliefs to your friend in words. Then you will have to rely on your study of the Faith, which you will have been keeping continually fresh, and on the inspiration of the Holy Spirit. Pray before you say anything. Of course Britons have a reputation for finding any discussion of serious matters like religion difficult or embarrassing. Cardinal Newman, when defining the Victorian gentleman, characterised him as one who never inflicts pain, who carefully avoids whatever may cause a jar or jolt. Some Britons preserve such views today.

But apostolate with friends requires some risks. You also need to be optimistic that what you say and do is for the best, even if it does give a jolt. You are only doing what God wants for them. You need, however, to be prepared to accept an initial rebuff. Provided a friend is clear that anything you say about the Faith, or do because of it, is done out of human kindness and respect for them, they will, in the end, be grateful for what you do. But it may take a little time—sometimes even years—for this to be realised. Apostolate requires patience, and imagination. If one approach is unsuccessful, try another. Each soul may need a different approach.

Where should your field of apostolate be? Of course God may call some of you to a special vocation: to the priesthood, to be a member of a religious community, to work in a lay capacity in a Catholic school, or in community or missionary work, where the Church makes an open and specifically Catholic commitment. If so, your field of apostolate is, to some extent, defined for you. But for most of us our field of apostolate is to be found among our friends and colleagues at work. It is here that we need to use our talents.

With them, you need to decide when it is appropriate to say something about your Faith, when to affirm what you know to be right, even if it is not the view of the world (or the media!). You also need to decide when it is right to be prudent, and to be able to distinguish this from being cowardly. A different approach may be needed if you are seeking to bring someone back to the Faith, from the one you use if you are sowing a new seed. Even more difficult is the responsibility you have for telling a friend or colleague when they are acting against God's law by doing wrong. In our permissive age this is something which is frequently shirked. Many let their friends stumble or fall without a word. This is not true friendship at all; it lets our friend down, and weakens our own resistance to evil. Like children, we all need correction at times. But it is only when our friends or colleagues have confidence in us and our judgement, that we will be able to perform this important task effectively.

It is often the little things we can do or say at moments when our friend or colleague is in sorrow, or difficulty, that will be helpful both in human and spiritual terms. Watch and pray for opportunities. And do not be afraid to seek the help of other Catholics in your apostolic work. They may be able to help with their prayers, or their talents may be better suited to guiding your particular friend or colleague than yours. Remember that it is the glory of God and the saving of souls which is the task. If you prepare the ground, or even sow the seed, it may be for others to help God reap the harvest. That is all part of the wonderfully co-operative nature of the apostolate, and the building up of God's Church.

Heaverham, Kent

CHAPTER SIX

GO IN PEACE

WE HAVE come on a long pilgrimage together. I pray that some of you may now make your way further along the path which leads to a safe haven. I hope that in any case we are still friends.

Christian friendship is a great blessing. To preserve it, as that great 12th century Cistercian monk from Yorkshire, St Ælred, reminds us, all we need is that God is the third person in the friendship. When He is continually present, there is little chance that we can inadvertently harm each other. I pray that this will always be the case in the friendship I hope we have built, albeit at a distance.

As I was completing this book I came across *The Wayfarers' Journal* by John Lloyd and Pat Sellars. It was published in 1991. On the surface it is a record of the journeys of a small company of men whose recreation is walking together in the British countryside, enjoying the rural scenery, visiting its churches, inns and ancient monuments. One of their company is a calligrapher, so the book is beautifully illuminated, and there are maps and drawings of the routes they took and what they saw. Even if you are not a walker, I would urge all of you to seek it out. For there is a spiritual dimension to their journeys: one of their company is a Catholic priest who acts as their chaplain. Someone like me, who has been travelling much of his life, can see the significance of that.

But the book also celebrates friendship, its loyalty, its joy and its humour. There is a little of St Francis of Assisi about it. These friends have been walking together regularly for over thirty years. Such loyalty and friendship warms the heart. For me it is a reflection of what Our Lord is continually offering us all in His Church, that Pearl of Great Price.

Strathglass

1. V. The angel of the Lord declared unto Mary:
R. And she conceived by the Holy Ghost.

Hail Mary, full of grace, the Lord is with thee; blessed art thou among women, and blessed is the fruit of thy womb, Jesus. Holy Mary, mother of God, pray for us sinners, now and at the hour of our death. Amen.

2. V. Behold the handmaid of the Lord:
R. Be it done unto me according to thy word.
Hail Mary &c.

3. V. And the Word was made flesh:
R. And dwelt among us.
Hail Mary &c.

4. V. Pray for us, O holy Mother of God:

R. That we may be made worthy of the promises of Christ.

5. V. Pour forth, we beseech thee, O Lord, thy grace into our hearts, that we, to whom the incarnation of Christ was made known by the message of an angel, may by His Passion and Cross, be brought to the glory of His resurrection, through the same Christ our Lord.
R. Amen.

6. V. May the divine assistance remain always with us and may the souls of the faithful departed, through the mercy of God, rest in peace. R. Amen.

I. V. Angelus Domini nuntiavit Mariæ:
R. Et concepit de Spirito Sancto.

Ave, Maria, gratia plena, Dominus tecum; benedicta tu in mulieribus, et benedictus fructus ventris tui; Jesus. Sancta Maria, mater Dei, ora pro nobis peccatoribis, nunc et in hora mortis nostræ.
Amen.

II. V. Ecce ancilla Domini.

R. Fiat mihi secundum verbum tuum.
Ave, Maria &c

III. V. Et verbum caro factum est.
R. Et habitavit in nobis.
Ave, Maria &c

IV. V. Ora pro nobis, sancta Dei Genetrix:
R. Ut digni efficiamur promissionibus Christi.

V. V. Gratiam tuam quæsumus, Domine, mentibus nostris infunde. ut qui, angelo nuntiante, Christi filii tui Incarnationem, cognovimus, per Passionem Ejus et crucem ad Resurrectionis gloriam perducamur. Per eundem Christum, Dominum nostrum.
R. Amen.

VI. V. Divinum auxilium maneat semper nobiscum, et fidelium animæ per misericordiam Dei requiescant in pace.
R. Amen

BOOKS MENTIONED

(Alphabetical according to the surname of the author or publisher)

Donald Attwater, *A Dictionary of Saints* (London 1965)

Hilaire Belloc, *The Path to Rome* (London 1902)

Robert Hugh Benson, *Confessions of a Convert* (London 1913)

Cecilia Bevan, *A Book of Catholic Prayers* (Wells 1987)

Edwin Burton, *The Life and Times of Bishop Challoner* 1691-1781 (London 1909)

Catholic Truth Society, *A Catechism of Christian Doctrine* (London 1985); *A Simple Prayer Book* (London 1986); *The Order of the Mass in Latin and English* (London 1977)

Richard Challoner, *Garden of the Soul* (London 1740, but there are many revised editions)

G K Chesterton, *Chaucer* (London 1932); *Autobiography* (London 1936)

Kenelm Digby, *The Broadstone of Honour* (London 1822); *Mores Catholici* (London 1831-42); *Compitum* (London 1849-54); *The Chapel of St John* (London 1861)

Four Courts Press, *The Navarre Bible* (Dublin; all the books of *The New Testament* are in the process of being published separately)

Monsignor Alfred Gilbey, *We Believe* (London 1983)

Alec Guinness, *Blessings in Disguise* (London 1985)

Ronald Knox, *A Spiritual Æneid* (London 1918); *Retreat in Slow Motion* (London 1960); with **Arnold Lunn**, *Difficulties* (London 1932); *Enthusiasm* (London 1950)

John Lloyd and Pat Sellars, *The Wayfarers' Journal* (London 1991)

Dom Gerard MacGinty OSB, *Today We Celebrate* (London 1986)

Malcolm Muggeridge, *Conversion - A Spiritual Journey* (London 1988)

Blessed John Henry Newman, *Essay on the Development of Christian Doctrine* (London 1846); *Loss and Gain* (London 1848); *Callista* (London 1856); *Apologia Pro Vita Sua* (London 1864) *An Essay in Aid of a Grammar of Assent* (London 1870)

Sceptre Ltd, *Daily Roman Missal* (London 1989)

George N Schuster, *The Catholic Spirit in Modern English Literature* (New York 1922)

Robert Speaight, *The Property Basket* (London 1970)

Francis Thompson, *The Poems of Francis Thompson* (London 1913)

Reverend Hugh Thwaites SJ, *The Talking Catechism*, a commentary on tape on *A Catechism of Christian Doctrine*. (Christus Vincit Productions. PO Box 17, Rainham, Gillingham, Kent ME8 0JU)

Evelyn Waugh, *Brideshead Revisited* (London 1945); *The Life of the Right Reverend Ronald Knox* (London 1959); *A Little Learning: The First Volume of an Autobiography* (London 1964)

Also from the Fisher Press:

CONFESSIONS OF A CONVERT

Robert Hugh Benson

R H Benson was the youngest son of one of the most extraordinary literary families of this century. Edward Benson, his father, was Archbishop of Canterbury and a pillar of the Victorian establishment. All three of his sons became writers. The eldest, A C Benson was a prominent biographer, diarist and literary critic. The second son, E F Benson, also wrote prolifically: his satirical Mapp and Lucia novels are now recognised as comic masterpieces, and have been the subject of a successful television series.

The youngest was in many ways the most fascinating. After taking Holy Orders in the Church of England to please his father, he caused a national sensation by becoming a Roman Catholic, and then a Catholic priest.

Between his conversion in 1903, and his death in 1914 at the early age of 43, R H Benson, while continuing to exercise his priestly vocation, wrote fifteen novels. Most were best-sellers. They included five historical novels about Tudor and Jacobean England, a mediæval romance, seven novels about the life and dilemmas of Edwardian society, and two prophetic novels about the future of England and Europe. Aspects of the last two foreshadow Huxley's Brave New World and Orwell's 1984. Benson also wrote ghost stories, plays, sermons and poetry. The income from this huge literary output enabled him to buy a large country house in Hertfordshire which he left in his will to the Catholic Archbishops of Westminster. It is still used by Cardinal Hume as a country retreat today.

R H Benson's autobiographical memoir is a classic story of religious conversion. He recounts how he gradually came to see that he had no other intellectual choice but to become a Catholic. His concerns about the nature of the Anglican Church, and the direction it was then taking are similar to those which many Anglicans feel today. But as the son of an Anglican Archbishop, whom he greatly admired, he had to overcome major emotional and social difficulties in following the path he knew to be right. The story of his intellectual and spiritual progress is told with great Bensonian charm; and there are splendid vignettes of his Edwardian contemporaries and his formidable family who were looking on as he prepared to take his momentous decision.

129x198mm 128 pages ISBN 1 874037 00 0
wood-free paper £4.99

If you have difficulty in obtaining Fisher Press books from your local bookshop, you can obtain these direct from Fisher Press, Post Office Box 41, Sevenoaks, Kent TN13 6YN, England.